THE POWER OF GRATITUDE

365 DAILY DEVOTIONS

BroadStreet
PUBLISHING

BroadStreet Publishing Group, LLC.
Savage, Minnesota, USA
Broadstreetpublishing.com

THE POWER OF GRATITUDE

© 2024 by BroadStreet Publishing®

9781424566938
9781424566945 (eBook)

Devotional entries composed by Sara Perry.

Typesetting and design by Garborg Design Works | garborgdesign.com
Editorial services by Michelle Winger | literallyprecise.com and Carole Holdahl

Printed in China.

24 25 26 27 28 29 30   7 6 5 4 3 2 1

Since we are receiving
a kingdom that cannot
be shaken, let us be thankful,
and so worship God acceptably
with reverence and awe.

HEBREWS 12:28-29
NIV

INTRODUCTION

Gratitude is a powerful weapon against toxic emotions like envy, resentment, and frustration. Being grateful also improves physical and relational health, helping individuals boost self-esteem and decrease self-pity. When people focus on the things they are grateful for, their satisfaction in life increases. Comparisons cease. Unnecessary pursuits pause. And they begin to notice things that truly matter. Life. Breath. Generosity. Beauty. Grace. This is where deep connection with God is found.

As you read these devotions and Scriptures, be inspired to live with gratitude in your heart and praise on your lips. Meditate on things that produce life and peace. Evaluate each day in the light of God's truth and stand in awe of a heavenly Father who gives abundantly more than you can ask or imagine. As you quiet yourself before him, experience the goodness of his presence and be refreshed with his life-giving joy.

Choose to be thankful today and watch how it changes your perspective for the days ahead.

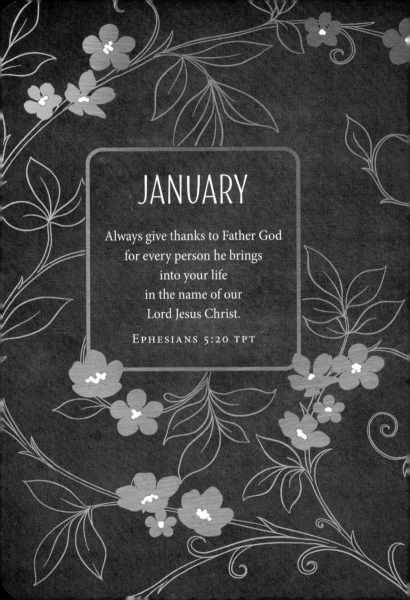

JANUARY

Always give thanks to Father God
for every person he brings
into your life
in the name of our
Lord Jesus Christ.

EPHESIANS 5:20 TPT

COURAGEOUS GRATITUDE

"Be strong and courageous, and do the work. Don't be afraid or discouraged, for the LORD God, my God, is with you. He will not fail you or forsake you. He will see to it that all the work related to the Temple of the LORD is finished."

1 CHRONICLES 28:20 NLT

The practice of gratitude has many benefits to our overall well-being. Studies now show that our relationships, our mental and physical health, and our life satisfaction are all boosted as we incorporate this practice into our daily lives. Gratitude helps us to be grounded in the present moment, in what is true here and now. Sure, it won't erase the challenges, but it can help us to be resilient in them as we see that the challenges are not the only part of our lives.

It takes courage to stand rooted in the present and to look for the goodness that is with us now. The smile of a stranger, the hug of a loved one, a warm home, and food on the table—the simplest things can be a perfect place to start. Gratitude may feel like work at first, but the more you practice it, the more you will build that muscle and create new neural pathways that make it feel easier over time!

Start a journal. Call it your Gratitude Journal and list in it a few things you are grateful for every day.

LIFE-GIVING FRIENDS

I have not stopped giving thanks for you,
remembering you in my prayers.

EPHESIANS 1:16 NIV

When we take time to be grateful for the people in our lives, evidence shows that our social bonds grow stronger. When we can pinpoint the qualities which we are thankful for in the people around us, we are more compelled to treat them as gifts. It can be easy to get caught up in frustrations, but what if we spent just as much energy or even more on what we are grateful for?

Think about the people in your life you are grateful for and why. Don't just shrug off this exercise if nothing comes to mind at first. Think of those closest to you. What are the attributes in them that you appreciate? As you begin to recognize what those qualities are, take note of them. The next time you see them, make a point of sharing those thoughts with them. We can't take for granted that our loved ones know what we appreciate about them. Let's be intentional and make sure they know!

Tell at least two people in your life what you are grateful for about them today no matter how insignificant it might seem to you. It just may be the encouragement they need.

IN THE WAITING

The LORD will wait, that He may be gracious to you;
And therefore He will be exalted,
that He may have mercy on you.
For the LORD is a God of justice;
Blessed are all those who wait for Him.

ISAIAH 30:18 NKJV

How many of us find it easy to dream about what we will be grateful for in the future? Any dream, hope, or longing is easy to conjure up. Yet, if we spend too much time on the *not yet* we may miss the enjoyment of the *now*. We are blessed in the waiting—read the last part of today's verse once more. There are reasons to be thankful today no matter where you are or what you are facing.

Waiting doesn't have to be boring or painful. We truly can learn to enjoy the slower pace in the in-between periods. We don't have to ignore the longing we feel in the waiting. However, when we shift our perspective to what is true, what is good, and what is precious in the present, we expand our awareness of the presence of God with us. God is so gracious, and his grace is abundant toward us today.

Pay attention to the little things that make you feel connected to the present today.

SPEAKING TRUTH

"When the Spirit of truth comes,
he will guide you into all truth.
He will not speak on his own
but will tell you what he has heard."

JOHN 16:13 NLT

Truth need not be harsh nor sweet. It is simply that which is true and remains true whether we acknowledge it or not. We don't have to ignore reality, our experiences, or the experiences of others in order to uphold it. It stands regardless.

When we learn to recognize the truth for what it is, gratitude can play a part in our response. Think of the promises of the Lord, in particular his promise that he will never leave us nor forsake us. He will come again and make all wrong things right. He is full of mercy toward us. That is the truth we stand upon. Even with truths that seem overwhelming or unpleasant, our gratitude can be shown in how we choose to respond. We are not powerless, for our agency is always available. Let's partner with the Lord and his truth and follow his lead of love as we live our lives.

Meditate on the promises of God and pray them back to him with a thankful heart.

SHARE YOUR GRATITUDE

"Go back to your home, and tell all that God has done for you." And off he went, proclaiming throughout the town how much Jesus had done for him.

LUKE 8:39 CSB

There is power in our testimonies of God's faithfulness. There is encouragement for others in our own breakthroughs. Our gratitude can inspire others to look for reasons to be grateful in their own lives. Think of a time when you were encouraged by the story of what God did for someone. God meets us each where we are, and he moves with mercy in each of our lives though the details will look different for each person.

Sharing our hearts with one another connects us. When we grieve with each other or when we celebrate with one another, we are showing the support found in a connective community. We were made to lean on each other. None of us is perfect, though we are all worthy of authentic relationships. Consider what you can share with a friend today. Simply tell them what God has done for you!

Share good news—and it doesn't have to be new—with someone today.

HEART OF PRAISE

Bless the LORD, O my soul,
and all that is within me,
bless his holy name!
Bless the LORD, O my soul,
and forget not all his benefits.

PSALM 103:1-2 ESV

As we focus on the goodness of the Lord and his faithful nature and kindness toward us, our hearts will expand in response. As our hearts expand in awe, they will overflow with thankfulness and praise.

When we begin our days with hearts attuned to the wonder of God, his creation, and the gift of life, we can't help but thank him. We can intentionally build this practice of focused praise in our lives. As humans, we are prone to focusing on negative things; the harsher realities of life are everywhere. Still, there is evidence that as we engage with the goodness in our own lives, as we purposely looking for gifts in the simplest of places, we can train our brains to look for these more and more. What an invitation this is to turn our hearts in praise to our Maker today.

Spend time in prayer thanking God for specific things you are thankful for.

BOOST OF CONFIDENCE

What should we say then?
Since God is on our side,
who can be against us?

ROMANS 8:31 NCV

Studies show that as we ground ourselves in the present moment and focus on what is good, there are multiple benefits to our mental and emotional health. One of those benefits is self-confidence. If we want to feel better about ourselves, we can start by seeing the beauty of life and the world around us, as well as our place in it.

You were thoughtfully created in the image of your maker, and he doesn't make mistakes. He knit you together with purpose and delight. If he delights in you, why shouldn't you? You are wonderfully made, and God loves you just as you are; that will always be true. You cannot convince him out of his love for you, so why not try seeing yourself from his perspective? Stand in confidence that you are loved, you are accepted, and you belong in his kingdom.

Make a list of everything you like about yourself and when you're feeling down, read it.

THINGS THAT MATTER

The kingdom of God is not eating and drinking,
but righteousness and peace and joy in the Holy Spirit.

ROMANS 14:17 NASB

We can get so easily distracted by silly things that don't really matter in the long run. Some call that "getting lost in the weeds." When we do this, we lose sight of the bigger picture, and maybe even forget the things that we value the most.

There are opportunities in every area of our lives to refocus and refine our visions. As we intentionally define the values we want to live by, we can evaluate how to refocus our energy spent in terms of time, attention, etc. in order to support these values. At the same time, we can choose to give less time to things that pull us away from them. God is full of wisdom, and he will offer insight when we ask him. Let's not forget to pull him into the process and ask his Spirit to reveal how we can put this into practice. Don't forget that the fruit of the Spirit is how we measure success in the kingdom, not what we eat, drink, or wear!

Take some time to think through what is most important to you in this season of your life. Write down ways you can focus on those qualities in your lifestyle choices.

ASTOUNDING KINDNESS

Yahweh is always good and ready to receive you.
He's so loving that it will amaze you—
so kind that it will astound you!

PSALM 100:5 TPT

It costs us nothing to be kind to one another, except perhaps our pride and patience. God is incredibly kind with us, and we can choose to act that way with one another. When we interact with others graciously, we make room for whatever is going on in their lives while offering respect. If we want to be like Jesus, we cannot overlook the very practical area of how we treat one another.

Consider how someone else's kind act toward you made you feel. We have all received kindness in one way or another. In fact, we probably have known it in a myriad of ways. Kindness can go a long way in building relationships, but it also makes us feel better about ourselves when we choose to be kind.

Find ways to extend kindness to others today and reflect on how it felt to make that choice purposefully.

LOVED TO LIFE

"The Father himself loves you."

JOHN 16:27 NIV

There is an inherent confidence and unshakable peace that comes with being seen, known, and loved. What a gift it is. There is little in this life more important than the relationships we have with those we love. May we not take them for granted!

There are people in your life who love you and those whom you love. Apart from that, there is a God who created you in love. Love is at the center of creation, for it is the very essence of God. Knowing this, our very grateful response can be to move in love today. First John 4:7 says, "Dear friends, let us love one another, for love comes from God. Everyone who loves has been born of God and knows God." Love is practical, generous, and life-giving. Choosing love may mean laying down our own preferences at times, but it is worth it in order to have a glimpse into God's own love.

When you recognize something done out of love, thank the person for it. Let love move you into action toward others today.

GIFTS OF GRACE

By grace you have been saved through faith,
and that not of yourselves; it is the gift of God.

EPHESIANS 2:8 NKJV

Grace is not something we can earn. It is extended. It is the gift of God. We can choose to give grace to others just as God does. When we would normally jump to conclusions or react in frustration, what would it look like instead to slow down and give grace?

The more aware we are of the grace we receive, the easier it is to extend it to others. It is wise, then, to allow ourselves to see the areas of our own weaknesses. What grace there is for us to be human, to err, and to make some efforts to repair the damage that we do. Let's take perfection off the table in our own estimation of ourselves, as well as in our expectations of others. As we do, we create the space for grace.

When you are tempted to jump to conclusions, choose to slow down and make space for grace. Instead of accusing, ask questions. Instead of rushing on, take time to really see what's going on.

GOD KEEPS RECORD

"Nothing is hidden that will not be made manifest, nor is anything secret that will not be known and come to light."

LUKE 8:17 ESV

Part of our gratitude in our relationships with the Lord is the very fact that we are not responsible for what we do not know or what we cannot do. This does not mean that we don't transform as we grow, but it does mean that we rest in his infinite wisdom and leadership. He keeps record of what others forget. He never misses a detail.

Knowing this, we can trust him in his faithfulness to do what needs to be done. Let's step back from feeling the need to control outcomes and instead rest in his ability to do more than we can ask or even imagine. When it's time to partner with him in action, we can do it. But the rest of the story? The rest we leave to him. We cast our cares on him, and he cares for us. There's no need to worry because he is the God of solutions, and he is never confused.

If you find yourself unable to shake anxiety or worry, write down the specific things that are on your mind and offer them to God in prayer. As you do, remember that he can handle it, and you don't have to carry that weight.

COMFORT AND RELIEF

Your promise revives me;
it comforts me in all my troubles.

PSALM 119:50 NLT

Sorrow and grief cannot be escaped in this life. They will enter our lives no matter what we do to try to avoid them. We can't pretend that they don't exist. It is not a failure to be sad, and it is not a lack of faith to grieve what is lost. Jesus grieved, and so will you. Gratitude is not in the absence of pain, but in the presence of goodness.

Even a tiny comfort can feel like a brief reprieve to a sorrow-burdened soul. The relief that comfort brings is beautiful. It doesn't mask the pain, but it acknowledges that good and bad can coexist. Hard times and peace are not mutually exclusive. Even in the darkest moments of our lives, there is still something to grasp that is sturdy, true, and unchangeable. May we not lose sight of this but see it for the gift that it is.

When you are overwhelmed by hard feelings, don't deny them. Instead, look for ways to touch them in the present moment. Can you be thankful for the ground that holds you up and for the air that meets your nostrils and fills your lungs?

BEYOND ACCOMPLISHMENTS

He saved us, not on the basis of deeds which we did in righteousness, but in accordance with His mercy, by the washing of regeneration and renewing by the Holy Spirit.

TITUS 3:5 NASB

There are probably things that you have accomplished in this life of which you are proud. These are to be celebrated. However, there are also good things in your life which you did nothing to earn. Where you grew up, who your family is, and other situational realities are not badges of honor that you earned. They don't reflect your worth. They are simply where you were placed.

This may feel like a mixed bag, to identify the things in your life that have nothing to do with your choices. Still, this is much like the work of mercy. There may be some hard realities you have had to contend with, but there are also gifts you have been given. Spend time today looking for those gifts that are imprints of the Lord's mercy on your life. You may be surprised by what you find!

Make a list of things you are grateful for that you could not choose nor earn.

SLOW TO ANGER

The LORD passed in front of him and proclaimed: The LORD—the LORD is a compassionate and gracious God, slow to anger and abounding in faithful love and truth.

EXODUS 34:6 CSB

Gratitude has been shown to increase patience in those who practice it. Perhaps because gratitude forces us to be more present in our lives rather than trying to escape it, we can see the benefit of patience. When we are on edge, anger is closer to the surface. It may not take much to set us off. However, when we have some margins, there is room to take things a bit slower. When we are not in a rush, there is a tendency toward calm.

We all have issues in our lives that we want to improve. For some of us, that includes wanting to be more patient with those we love. One practical way to do this is to practice gratitude. As we do, our minds create pathways for more reasons to be grateful, and this happens in real time. God is patient and slow to anger with us and thank goodness he is. Gratitude can help us become more like him.

When you feel yourself getting angry, step back for a moment, take a deep breath and remind yourself of something that you are grateful for directly in that moment.

LED BY WONDER

Jesus called for the children, saying, "Let the little children come to me. Don't stop them, because the kingdom of God belongs to people who are like these children."

LUKE 18:16 NCV

One practical way to find gratitude in our hearts is to allow childlike awe and wonder to lead our thoughts. What are the things that stop us in our tracks? It may help to consider what fascinated us as children. Play is as important to adults as it is for children. It has been shown to boost creativity, sharpen the sense of humor, and make it easier to learn a new task.

The seriousness of life cannot be escaped, but it also doesn't need to be engaged all the time. Play helps us focus where we're at in the moment, just as gratitude does. It is not a prescriptive thing either—it will look unique to each of us. What did you love playing as a kid? Perhaps you can allow your inner child to do that today. It's not frivolous to spend time enjoying yourself! If Jesus encouraged the children to come to him, you can remember that you are God's child and therefore act accordingly.

Do something simply for the fun of it today. Allow yourself to feel the delight of play.

FOUNDATIONAL PRAYERS

You know that I've been called to serve the God of my fathers with a clean conscience. Night and day I pray constantly for you, building a memorial for you with my prayers.

2 TIMOTHY 1:3 TPT

Prayer is a powerful tool for gratitude. In the process of letting go of what you cannot control, you allow your heart to open to what is true. As you pray for the best for others around you, you align yourself with heaven's heart for them. God is a good and loving Father, and he loves to help his children. We can partner with his heart as we pray for him to bring about breakthroughs for one another.

James 5:16 says that "tremendous power is released through the passionate heartfelt prayer of a godly believer!" Don't overlook the power to build both your own faith the faith of those around you with your bold prayers for freedom, provision, and breakthrough. Constant prayer can be happening in your heart as you keep it open in love, concern, and care, no matter where you are or who you are with.

Pick someone to pray for throughout your day. Whenever you think of them, thank God for them and say a prayer on their behalf.

SATISFIED

"The Lord will guide you always;
he will satisfy your needs in a sun-scorched land
and will strengthen your frame.
You will be like a well-watered garden,
like a spring whose waters never fail."

ISAIAH 58:11 NIV

One of the extraordinary benefits of gratitude is that is causes a rise in our overall satisfaction with our lives. As we recognize what we once overlooked and we appreciate the things we have taken for granted, we realize that there is goodness all around us. There is beauty in the lives we now live. We don't have to wish for the future because we are grounded in the gift of the present.

Today is all that we have. The choices we make now will inform each moment as we continue to live. It's up to us, then, to choose this day how we will live. Not only that, but the ways we interact with the people in our lives and how we think about them is important in forming our perspectives. We can find great satisfaction as we open our eyes to the provision that is ours. We all have reasons to rejoice today!

Challenge yourself to look for the good in your life throughout the day.

SMALL BEGINNINGS

"Do not despise these small beginnings,
for the Lord rejoices to see the work begin."

ZECHARIAH 4:10 NLT

When we have big dreams in our hearts, the meager beginning steps toward those dreams can feel underwhelming. However, we don't get from a dream to a reality by simply continuing to dream. We must do the work. As we do, the plans become clearer and we can refine our path and our methods. What celebration there is in the implementation of a passion!

We become empowered as we do the work. The Lord is with us in every step. Recognizing that we are on the journey of God's intention can allow us to stop comparing our own purpose and where we are to others' paths. As we give our attention to what is ours to do, we can build gratitude for this moment, while recognizing that these current steps are also building for the future. Let's not despise our small beginnings, for the Lord rejoices with us as we start!

Refuse to compare your beginning to someone else's middle. Take one step toward the dream that you have in your heart and thank God that he rejoices with you as you start.

CONSIDER THE POSSIBILITIES

"With men this is impossible,
but with God all things are possible."

MATTHEW 19:26 NKJV

As we remember that all things are possible with God including what seems impossible to us, we refocus our perspectives on the power of God rather than ruminating on our own inabilities. One of the ways we can encourage this is to remember the hard situations we've already walked through. Where did our worries fall flat? Did we recognize that God provided for us in those past difficulties?

We can take courage for whatever we face through the faithfulness of God as we have witnessed throughout our own history. And God isn't tired or unimaginative. He can do much more than he has already done. Let's join our hopes to his power and our peace to his loyal love, for he can do far more than we can even imagine.

Instead of getting lost in the unknown, ground yourself in the gratitude of what God has already done for you, and look ahead with eyes of faith. Trust him fully to continue to take care of you.

CHEERFUL GIVING

Each person should do as he has decided in his heart—
not reluctantly or out of compulsion,
since God loves a cheerful giver.

2 CORINTHIANS 9:7 CSB

Gratitude makes our connection to compassion stronger. As we recognize what we must be thankful for in our lives, we are often compelled to give to others out of the charity in our hearts. We shouldn't give grudgingly as if we have no choice in the matter. We always have a choice!

Before we decide how we want to give back to our communities, let's remember the things that have been so meaningful to us. As we look back over our history and recognize the gifts that others have given us or the seeds that they have sown into us, we may be able to more clearly decide how we want to cheerfully give to others. What an honor it is to use our gratitude to serve others! It is a beautiful reflection of God's heart as we partner with his generosity.

Volunteer to give back in some way or consider giving financially to a cause that is meaningful to you.

BRIDGES OF PEACE

He himself is our peace, who has made us both one and has broken down in his flesh the dividing wall of hostility.

EPHESIANS 2:14 ESV

As we focus on that which we appreciate in our lives especially in our relationships, we are more drawn in grace toward one another. Offenses and walls of hostility keep us at a distance from one another. Love and gratitude draw us toward the other. Christ is our peace, and he is the ultimate peacemaker. He is the bridge between us and God, and his love can also bridge any gaps between us.

Gratitude strengthens our social bonds. This is so important to remember! If we are having trouble with impatience in our relationships, remembering what we love and appreciate about the person is a good place to start. Relationships are two-way streets; if someone doesn't respond well or at all, we can choose to adjust our own boundaries accordingly. However, let's be sure to do what we can to extend kindness and grace in order to do our own part as well as possible.

When you find yourself losing patience with someone close to you today, slow down, take a deep breath, and consider at least one thing you appreciate about them.

CONTINUAL KINDNESS

The LORD appeared to his people and said,
"I love you people
with a love that will last forever.
That is why I have continued
showing you kindness."

JEREMIAH 31:3 NCV

There is power in our gratitude. Our thankfulness toward another can have a positive effect on their actions. In the same way, when we are grateful for someone's kindness toward us, we may very well be driven to return that kindness. In short, kindness is contagious!

The Lord is the ultimate standard in loving-kindness. His love moves him in patience, mercy, grace, and peace. He offers us kindness after kindness. His mercies are new every morning. When we take time to recognize his kindness in the practical ways it shows up in our lives, we are quicker to return that kindness to him and to live that example in our lives. How different would our lives look if we ventured to outdo one another in kindness?

Take time to think of a specific kindness that was recently shown to you. Return it in kind today!

BLESSED CONSISTENCY

Jesus Christ is the same yesterday
and today and forever.

HEBREWS 13:8 NASB

Consistency is a powerful reflection of our integrity. When we are the same person with the people in our lives and we live by the same values and not change who we are based on who we are around, we reflect the security we have in our own identity. When we follow through on what we say we will do, or alternatively when we habitually don't, our consistency—or our lack thereof—is plain to those in our lives.

Consistency, kindness, and trustworthiness are strong character traits. They reveal a lot about a person. Consider what you are consistent about in your own life. Do you over-promise and under-deliver? If this is true, it may be time to reevaluate how much you commit to. None of us is superhuman, and we all have limits. It is not a failure to recognize them. Be grateful for what you can do and be honest about what you cannot. There is blessing in this!

Take an honest look at your commitments and consider cutting down on the ones that don't serve your values or priorities at this point in your life. It is better to do few things well than to overcommit and not do any of them well.

A LIFE OF PRAYER

Let joy be your continual feast. Make your life a prayer.
And in the midst of everything be always giving thanks,
for this is God's perfect plan for you in Christ Jesus.

1 THESSALONIANS 5:16-18 TPT

Make your life a prayer. That is what Paul advised in his
first letter to the Thessalonians. Pray without ceasing. That
is how many of us may more readily recognize this verse.
However, it's worded the idea is the same—each breath
can be a prayer. God can read our hearts as readily as he
can hear our words. Let's live as if our actions, our heart
postures, and our thoughts are all expressions of prayer to
our Maker.

Gratitude connects us to the goodness of God. As we give
thanks to God for who he is, what he has done, and what he
continues to do, it doesn't matter what our circumstances
are. He is faithful throughout them all. He never changes.
He is always loyal in love, and he is trustworthy through
every hill and valley of this life.

*Open your heart and intentionally offer God the gratitude
of your heart whenever you think of it today. Remember
who he is!*

REVELATIONS OF LOVE

No one has ever seen God. But if we love each other, God lives in us, and his love is brought to full expression in us.

1 JOHN 4:12 NLT

Acts of appreciation can show love to the people in our lives in practical ways. God's love lives in us when we love one another. That doesn't mean loving each other is always easy, but as we consider the attributes, we are grateful for in one another it helps to propel us to show it.

Think of someone in your life, anyone you are close to. Now consider the things about them that you appreciate. Do they do something that makes you feel loved and accepted? Do they do something to lighten your load? Perhaps you simply enjoy who they are; they bring light and laughter or support when you need it. These are revelations of love. As you choose to show your own appreciation in practical ways, you are choosing the path of love.

Show your appreciation to someone in your life in a way that they receive love. If you aren't sure what that is, consider returning a favor that they have shown you!

CONFIDENCE OUTSIDE OURSELVES

Know therefore that the LORD your God is God;
he is the faithful God, keeping his covenant of love
to a thousand generations of those who love him
and keep his commandments.

DEUTERONOMY 7:9 NIV

When we become too focused on ourselves—when we are overly focused on our pitfalls, our victories, etc.—we can lose sight of the goodness around us. There are people who keep their word, offer support for others' needs, or recognize the great beauty in the world around us. And through it all, above it all, is the faithful love of our Creator.

Pride can lead us to undervalue others and overvalue ourselves. The tricky thing is that a focus on perfectionism can do the same thing. When we are consumed by our failures, we fall into the same trap as those who feel superior to others. None of us is perfect, but we are all made in the image of God. We are loved no matter what we do. Let's take the pressure off and thank God for his faithful love that covers us all the time!

Make a list of things you are grateful for which have nothing to do with anything you could ever do or offer.

FRUIT OF OUR LIPS

By Him let us continually offer the sacrifice of praise to God, that is, the fruit of our lips, giving thanks to His name.

HEBREWS 13:15 NKJV

What we say matters. The fruit of our lips start as seeds in our hearts. As we choose to honor God with the gratitude we purposely cultivate, we make room for more thankfulness to grow. Studies have shown that gratitude leads to the production of "happy hormones." A boosted mood is just one of the benefits of this practice!

As we choose to give voice to what we are grateful for, we encourage ourselves to look for the good in our lives, and we also encourage others to do the same. Behaviors rub off on the ones we spend time with, so let's not forget how the fruit of our lips can affect those around us. It is a good practice for all of us to be intentional in our gratitude!

Say thank you often to those around you today, including the Lord. Be specific about what you're thankful for!

EMPOWERED BY TRUST

Those who trust in the LORD
will renew their strength;
they will soar on wings like eagles;
they will run and not become weary,
they will walk and not faint.

ISAIAH 40:31 CSB

One of the most liberating truths of following the Lord is that we don't have to rely on ourselves. When we are weak, we lean into his everlasting arms, and he upholds us. We can rest in him both in our weaknesses and in our strengths. If we trust in him, he renews our strength with his Spirit. Why should we strive to achieve something we were never meant to attain?

Gratitude helps us reset our perspectives and lighten our mental loads. We are often too preoccupied with what needs to be done and we put pressure on ourselves to never stop working. This is not how we were meant to live. As we recognize the important aspects of our lives and give what we can, we then leave space for rest, and we can trust God with all we cannot control. Instead of doing more, let's trust him more, and rest in his faithfulness and care.

As things come to mind of what must be done, write them down and only do what must be done today. Take time to rest and trust God with what wasn't accomplished.

THE POWER OF AGENCY

"No one takes it from me, but I lay it down of my own accord. I have authority to lay it down, and I have authority to take it up again. This charge I have received from my Father."

JOHN 10:18 NIV

It is incredibly important that we recognize our agency to choose. Jesus chose to lay his life down. We cannot choose how others will receive or respond to us, but we can certainly choose our own actions and reactions.

As we choose to look for things to be grateful for and appreciate what is meaningful and valuable to us, we take agency over our own attitudes. This is one of the most liberating realizations that we can have—that we can only take control over ourselves and not over others. As we cultivate compassion in our hearts and appreciation for what we have, we soften our relationship with ourselves and with others. Jesus is our great example, and even his submission was his own choice. We should not overlook the power of our autonomy.

When you feel stuck today, look for ways that you can choose what is right. You are always entitled to your voice and participation, even when that looks like submission.

REASON TO HOPE

I have hope
when I think of this:
The LORD's love never ends;
his mercies never stop.
They are new every morning.

LAMENTATIONS 3:21-23 NCV

Even when everything feels like it is falling apart, there is always fresh mercy available to us. God's love is never stale. We don't have to rely on his kindness to us yesterday to get us through today. He is present with us now in whatever difficulty we are facing, and that means that we can rely on his mercy to meet us in each moment.

Gratitude helps us to recognize the valuable things that we already have. Some of life's challenges are thrown at us and we have absolutely no control over them. Others come along as a result of our own choices. Whenever we acknowledge the beauty of something in our lives and give thanks for it, we have tangible things to which we can connect our trust and hope. The Lord's love is ever flowing, and it gives us reasons to be thankful and to hope over and over again.

Right where you are, ask the Lord to meet you with tangible mercy. As he reveals his love, give him thanks for the specific ways he meets you.

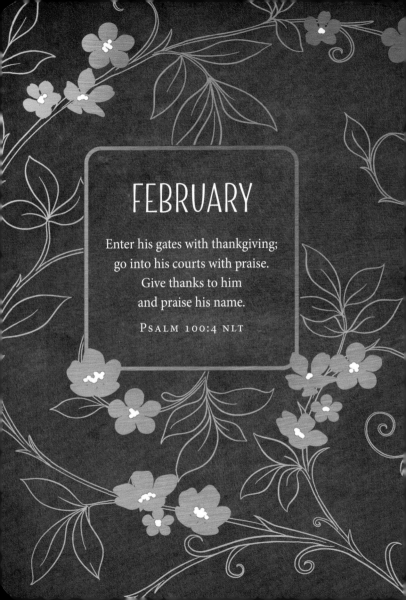

FEBRUARY

Enter his gates with thanksgiving;
go into his courts with praise.
Give thanks to him
and praise his name.

PSALM 100:4 NLT

COURAGE TO STAND

The Lord GOD helps Me,
Therefore, I am not disgraced;
Therefore, I have made My face like flint,
And I know that I will not be ashamed.

ISAIAH 50:7 NASB

When we are grounded in the truth of God's faithfulness, we partner with his presence and stand in courage. What a relief it is to know that God never leaves or forsakes us! He is with us, and knowing this, we can face whatever comes with the courage of a confident child who has only known the protection and power of a good and faithful father.

We will not be disgraced when we stand upon the truth and act in love. Let's be grateful for the fact that we never face anything alone—not one single thing in this life! The Lord God helps us. He helps us! What more do we need?

In the face of the what-ifs and the unknowns, remember that God is with you. He helps all those who call on him. Thank him for his help and trust him, and in the end, simply stand on his promises.

GROUNDED IN THE SPIRIT

God will never give you the spirit of fear,
but the Holy Spirit who gives you mighty power,
love, and self-control.

2 TIMOTHY 1:7 TPT

The Spirit of God does not punish us with shame, guilt, or fear. He reveals the heart of God to us and sows the seeds of his kingdom in our hearts and in our lives. If we are having a hard time deciphering the voice of God from our own inner ramblings, the response his voice elicits within us can help us distinguish between them. God's kindness which is always present, does not shy away from the truth, but it also does not beat us down in shame. It is often an invitation. He offers power, love, and self-control. He brings clarity rather than confusion.

God's Spirit does not force us to act. Rather, the Spirit offers wisdom which is grounded in who God is. What a good God he is, looking for partnership rather than blind obedience. We can trust him to handle us as we are, and we don't have to hide any part of ourselves from him. The Holy Spirit helps us; he does not barter in any tactics of manipulation. Thank God for that!

When you aren't sure of what God is saying to you, write it out. Then read it aloud. If what you read is aligned with God's character and it empowers you rather than diminishes you, thank him for speaking, and act on it.

JOY IS ACCESSIBLE

Our hearts ache, but we always have joy.
We are poor, but we give spiritual riches to others.
We own nothing, and yet we have everything.

2 CORINTHIANS 6:10 NLT

Joy is linked to gratitude. Gratitude as a practice helps us be more connected to goodness, which in turn gives us more satisfaction and joy in the day-to-day occurrences in our lives.

Gratitude requires us to slow down in the present and notice what we must be thankful for. If we want to be more joyful, then the place to start is by building a practice of gratitude. As we put habits in place to acknowledge the good around us, and then we follow through with them, it is almost guaranteed that our life's satisfaction and joy will increase.

Decide how you want your gratitude practice to look. Will you share something you are grateful for with your family at dinner? Will you write it down? Will you make a gratitude jar? Whatever feels attainable for you, decide and follow through with it.

CONTENT WITH TODAY

Be content with what you have, because God has said,
"Never will I leave you;
never will I forsake you."

HEBREWS 13:5 NIV

Contentment is inextricably linked to the present.
We cannot be content in yesterday or in tomorrow.
Contentment is found in the here and now. It is a gift when
we learn to be content with what we have without envy or
strife. This does not mean we abandon our goals, but our
life's satisfaction cannot be contingent upon things that we
do not yet have.

As we practice gratitude, we are actively thankful for what
we have. Contentment is satisfaction with what we have. If
we find our contentment lacking, practicing being grateful
for what we have can actively move us in that direction.
Now, there is a difference between trying to bypass
disappointment and true gratitude. We may not be thankful
to be going through a tough time, but chances are there are
details in our circumstances which we can be truly thankful
for. Let's look past the obvious and get into the specifics. In
those specifics, we may just cultivate the contentment we've
been missing!

*Write a list of everything you can think of that you are
honestly thankful for in your life—no matter how small
it seems.*

PERSISTENT HOPE

"There is hope for a tree,
If it is cut down, that it will sprout again,
And that its tender shoots will not cease."

JOB 14:7 NKJV

The kingdom of our God is a kingdom of redemption. Christ offers us new life for the endings in this life which we will face. He renews our minds, hearts, and bodies in the power of his mercy. There is no end that does not also have a new beginning in him. If there is hope for a tree to sprout again even after it has been cut down, then we, too, have that hope.

Even when all seems lost, it is not so. There is always hope. There is always faith and always love. Let's not give up in our despair, but instead look to the writer of our stories. He is faithful to lead us in a direction we did not know to go. He is dependable and true, no matter what is happening in our lives. Hope is persistent, and so is God. Let's persist in hope today, grounded in the goodness of God that is still with us!

In your disappointment, find a reason to still hope, no matter how small it may seem in the moment.

NO NEED TO STRIVE

"Don't strive for what you should eat
and what you should drink,
and don't be anxious."

LUKE 12:29 CSB

It is hard to find anyone these days who does not deal with some level of anxiety. Our world is full of reasons to worry, but God calls us to rest in him. Worry is wasted energy—we can't change a thing by fretting over it. When we choose to trust God with all that we cannot control, we can rest in his faithfulness.

We cannot escape having necessities in life, but we also don't need to strive so hard to meet those needs. There are many ways that God provides for us, and bringing together the creativity and partnership of others is just one way. One practical way to calm the anxiety in our minds and bodies is to take a few deep breaths, bringing our attention to the air around us and the ground beneath us. With a brief break, our minds can connect to where we are in this moment and trust that right here and now, we have all that we need.

Every time you are tempted to jump to the future and worry over what-ifs, take a deep breath, close your eyes, and thank God that you have all you need in this moment.

TRUSTWORTHY AND TRUE

"God is not man, that he should lie,
or a son of man, that he should change his mind.
Has he said, and will he not do it?
Or has he spoken, and will he not fulfill it?"

NUMBERS 23:19 ESV

Who are the dependable people in your life whom you can be thankful for? Even our dearest loved ones are not perfect, but we can certainly be grateful for who they are to us. When it all comes down to it, the Lord is the only perfect one. He never lies, never manipulates, and never misdirects. He faithfully fulfills all his promises!

If you find yourself discouraged by those who have let you down, it is okay to grieve that loss. But don't stop there! Remember who is there for you. Our friends and family are not mind readers. We must communicate our needs and expectations, and yes, even our disappointments. But we also should take time to express our gratitude.

Thank the dependable, honest, and loving people in your life today. Focus on the love you do have rather than the disappointment of what you do not.

CULTIVATING GRATITUDE

I will praise the LORD at all times;
his praise is always on my lips.

PSALM 34:1 NCV

Paying attention to the little things, the moments of pleasure, the glimpses of beauty, and the small kindnesses in our day can help us cultivate gratitude. If we approach the day with the intention of noticing the goodness no matter how simple or how grand it may be, we will be drawn to see it. This habit can lead to a positive, lasting impact on our overall health.

Gratitude is more than a fleeting feeling. When it is an actual, purposeful practice, it creates new neural pathways in our brains. We are never too old to learn new things, and that includes teaching our brains to look for the positives in life! It is not wishful thinking to focus on the good things in life. It is grounded in reality: it helps us connect to positive experiences rather than overlooking them in preference to negative ones. Let's honor our mental, physical, and emotional health and cultivate gratitude, not because we must, but because we can!

Pay attention to the little things today and give thanks for each of them!

ALWAYS A WAY

No temptation has overtaken you except something common to mankind; and God is faithful, so He will not allow you to be tempted beyond what you are able, but with the temptation will provide the way of escape also, so that you will be able to endure it.

1 CORINTHIANS 10:13 NASB

We are not stuck, even when we cannot see our way out of a situation. We always have something we can choose, even if it's just in our approach or attitude. The Lord promises to help us in our weakness, and this includes in our temptation to throw his way out and choose what may feel the easier path in the moment.

Gratitude helps us remember that goodness is always present. The ways of the Lord and the path of his love may feel harder to choose in the moment, but it is always the best way. We are never without a choice. Let's honor the Lord and our own autonomy as we choose to follow him, even when it costs us greatly.

Think about the last time you were tempted. Consider the different choices you could have made. No matter what you chose in the moment, consider the path of goodness and following God's ways. It may just help you the next time you're faced with another decision.

LAY IT DOWN

Pour out all your worries and stress upon him and leave
them there, for he always tenderly cares for you.

1 PETER 5:7 TPT

It is hard to be grateful when we're carrying the weight
of the world on our shoulders. We shouldn't pretend that
our worries are not there. Instead, we can offer them to
the Lord. We can lay them down before him as we tell him
what's weighing on our hearts and minds.

Instead of trying to positively think our way out of worry,
let's deal with the worry first, letting it go as we release it
to the Lord. Scripture says that we should "pour out all
your worries and stress upon him and leave them there."
When we do that, we can root ourselves in the reality of
his goodness and faithfulness which is with us now. There
is nothing too small to be an encouragement to our souls.
And through it all, we remember he always cares for us, and
he always takes good care of us.

*Before you go to bed tonight, write down every worry
and stress you have. Then release each of them to the Lord
as you pray.*

BEAUTIFUL GRACE

All of this is for your benefit. And as God's grace reaches
more and more people, there will be great thanksgiving,
and God will receive more and more glory.

2 CORINTHIANS 4:15 NLT

Gratitude is a beautiful trait that draws us to people.
Just think of those in your life whom you prefer to keep
your distance from. What are the characteristics of their
personalities? Do they focus on the negative too often? Now
consider the most genuinely grateful people you know. How
much more do you tend to want to spend time with them?

Grace and gratitude go hand in hand. Grace is a gift that we
do not deserve, given generously and without condition.
Gratitude is an acceptance of what good we have here and
now; it is not begging for more or focusing on what we lack.
Grace is enough in the moment. Gratitude asks us to see
that what we have is enough. Both are beautiful. Both are
endearing. May we choose to be gracious and grateful.

*Share your gratitude with those around you today and give
grace generously when you can.*

BEYOND THE SURFACE

"Let us acknowledge the LORD;
let us press on to acknowledge him.
As surely as the sun rises,
he will appear;
he will come to us like the winter rains,
like the spring rains that water the earth."

HOSEA 6:3 NIV

Acceptance can be a form of gratitude. While we recognize the season we are in, we also know that a new season will come. The rhythms of nature teach us that life is cyclical. Nothing except the Lord stays the same forever. We shift, grow, and change. That is good news in times of hardship.

Though the winter may feel barren, it is rich with rest. There are good and necessary things happening beyond the surface. We may need to dig a little, but we do we find that there is goodness here. No matter what season of life we find ourselves in, we can be sure that there is beauty within it. As we find that beauty, we can join it with the knowledge that a seasonal shift will also come. The faithfulness of God never fails.

Look beyond the face of your circumstances and dig a little deeper to uncover beauty and growth which you may have missed at first glance.

MINDFUL LIVING

Whether you eat or drink, or whatever you do,
do all to the glory of God.

1 CORINTHIANS 10:31 NKJV

Finding pleasure in the little things is as important to our gratitude as focusing on the big victories in our lives. In fact, it may be more impactful to our outlook overall. When we savor the cup of coffee as we start our days, or the way the fading light filters through our windows, or the sound of our loved ones' laughter of, these little delights become the highlights that mark our days.

What makes us happy is unique. What brings comfort is also subjective. Let's not ignore the way our hearts expand a little each time we engage with delight over the little things. The more we pay attention to these things, the more mindfully we engage with our lives. We can bring glory to God by learning to enjoy our lives as much as we do when we pray for him to have his way in them!

Notice the tastes, textures, and warmth you feel as you eat and drink today. Don't forget to enjoy even the necessities of life!

VOICE YOUR NEEDS

If any of you lacks wisdom, he should ask God—
who gives to all generously and ungrudgingly—
and it will be given to him.

JAMES 1:5 CSB

No one is an island. We were created for community, and we were made to lean on each other in times of need. Some needs go unmet because they are unknown to others. We cannot expect the close people in our lives to anticipate what we need if we are not willing to express it to them. It takes courage to voice a need, but it is a risk worth taking, especially with those we share our lives with.

God has solutions for our quandaries. When we don't know what to do, we should, as James said, ask God! In the same way that God gives generously and ungrudgingly, let's also honor the bids for help and connection from those we can support. We are the body of Christ, after all, and each of us plays a different part.

Instead of trying to do everything yourself today, ask someone for specific help in one area. If you find yourself on the receiving end of a request, do what you can to meet it!

FIND PEACE

"I have said these things to you, that in me you may have peace. In the world you will have tribulation. But take heart; I have overcome the world."

JOHN 16:33 ESV

When peace evades our souls, we should check in to see what is swirling around in our minds and hearts. What circumstances are we facing? What kinds of things have we been listening to and watching? As we look at our lives with curiosity, we can also take time to disconnect from the things that keep the chaos building and churning. Perhaps we need a break from social media or the news. Rest is available to each of us, but sometimes we need to protect it.

The same Jesus who slept peacefully during a harsh storm offers you the peace of his presence. He was not worried about the crashing waves. He knew they would make it through the storm. Join your heart to his faithfulness, and trust God with what you cannot control. Rest in him and be refreshed in his presence today.

When you feel overwhelmed by worry and anxiety, do something to ground yourself in the safety of the moment—a chat with a beloved friend, a warm bath, an afternoon nap—whatever works for you!

GREAT GENEROSITY

You are rich in everything—in faith, in speaking,
in knowledge, in truly wanting to help, and in the love
you learned from us. In the same way,
be strong also in the grace of giving.

2 CORINTHIANS 8:7 NCV

The more aware we are of the things in our life which we can be grateful for and the abundance we enjoy, the more freely we can be generous with our resources. Why wouldn't we share what we have with those who have less? It reflects Christ's love which is alive in us when we act as he would act.

The practice of gracious giving is directly tied to the level of gratitude we have for our blessings. Our gratitude points out where we have more than enough, so there is no need to approach our giving with any fear of scarcity. Whether we share meals, money, or time, it is important that we find ways to serve our communities. Generosity benefits everyone!

Recall some of the specific things you are grateful for in your life and spot where there is abundance. In those areas, how can you give back to others?

REFLECTIONS OF OUR FATHER

Whatever you do in word or deed,
do everything in the name of the Lord Jesus,
giving thanks through Him to God the Father.

COLOSSIANS 3:17 NASB

If we truly want to be reflections of Christ as we live our lives, we must account for how he would act. As we interact with our coworkers, build toward our futures, and care for our friends and family, we should do it all in the name of Jesus. We need to be mindful of how Christ loved those he walked with.

What an honor it is to choose how we live. There is so much grace for redirection and repentance. Let's give thanks to God for the chances we have before him to act as he would have us act, in mercy, kindness, and compassion, and in justice, liberation, and gracious generosity. What are you particularly grateful to Christ for today? How has his love affected your sense of being and belonging? However, he has transformed you for the better, try reflecting that to others by offering the same kindnesses.

Consider how you can reveal the love of Christ to those in your life today. Give thanks to God that you get to reflect what he has already shown you.

SO VERY ACCESSIBLE

The Messiah has come to preach this sweet message of peace
to you, the ones who were distant, and to those who are near.

EPHESIANS 2:17 TPT

Gratitude is linked to what is true here and now. It is having
the awareness to notice the good that is accessible to us in
the moment. It can certainly reflect our thankfulness for the
past and our hopes for the future, but it inherently connects
us to the present.

The all-surpassing peace of God is available to each of us
right now. It is available to all people distant and near. This
means no matter where you are, what you've done, or how
far you feel from God, his palpable peace is available to you.
Peace with God is not something we have to attain or earn.
It is offered to us through Christ. This is always true. It is a
gift of his grace. We simply need to receive it.

*Receive the gift of peace offered to you in the presence of
Christ today. Offer peace to those who need it as you interact
with others.*

STRENGTH AND ENDURANCE

The Sovereign LORD is my strength!
He makes me as surefooted as a deer,
able to tread upon the heights.

HABAKKUK 3:19 NLT

Gratitude has been shown to increase our emotional resilience. If we can become more capable of enduring whatever comes in life with the ease of a joyful and thankful heart, we can truly do anything. Gratitude leads to strength which leads back to gratitude. It's a cycle that builds our resilience and increases our joy.

Everything feels harder when we are weighed down by sorrow. This is not to say that we can escape loss or grief in this life. However, we can learn to find the goodness in it even in the hard times. We don't have to dismiss how hard life is in order to find beauty at the same time. Both can be true! As we practice gratitude, our resilience strengthens in the same way our muscles grow as we train them over time.

For every hard thing you see or face today, also take time to name something you are grateful for.

WHAT REMAINS

"Though the mountains be shaken
and the hills be removed,
yet my unfailing love for you will not be shaken
nor my covenant of peace be removed,"
says the LORD, who has compassion on you.

ISAIAH 54:10 NIV

When the world is shaking and your life feels the effects of it, what remains? Though you may lose some things in the shaking, there are still some that remain and will continue to. It can be incredibly disorienting when we go through a major shaking in our lives. Sometimes this will be a collective experience like Covid-19 was. Other times it will feel lonely, like an illness or the death of a loved one.

It is important to not lose sight of what remains true. In these times of shaking, we can more readily see the importance of the little things which we may have taken for granted before. Take stock of the things that remain true, beautiful, and good. They are gifts that are ripe for your gratitude!

Savor one small thing today that you truly enjoy about your life. Thank God that there is goodness that remains, even when other things are lost.

TEACHABLE HEARTS

"The Helper, the Holy Spirit, whom the Father will send in My name, He will teach you all things, and bring to your remembrance all things that I said to you."

JOHN 14:26 NKJV

We are never without help. The Holy Spirit is always a ready helper. With all the wisdom of God, he reminds us of the Word of God and reveals the deep truths of his kingdom. We cannot presume to have it all figured out in any area of life. We are all learning until the day we die, or at least we should be.

We can only know what we know, so we shouldn't beat ourselves up for our mistakes in the past. However, when we know better, we should act accordingly and do better. As we keep our hearts humble and open, we can more easily learn the lessons and realities of other perspectives than we do when we resist them. A teachable heart is one that admits it doesn't know it all. Pride goes before a fall, as the proverb goes, but those who are open to redirection will not be tripped up when it happens to them.

As an act of gratitude, be willing to learn something new today whether it is a different perspective or a new way of doing something. Be sure to thank the person who teaches you!

SEEK AND YOU WILL FIND

"Blessed are those who hunger and thirst for righteousness,
for they will be filled."

MATTHEW 5:6 CSB

What we focus on matters. If we expect to be disappointed,
we will find reasons to be so. If we look for the beauty
around us, we will also find that. Our minds are primed by
what we put our attention into. If we are more prone to look
for the negatives, we can still retrain our brains to look for
the positives, even amidst the harsh realities of life.

Jesus said that those who hunger and thirst for
righteousness will be filled. The intentions of our hearts
direct us to find what we are looking for. In Christ, we find
fullness. In him, we find our peace and our salvation. This
does not mean our lives are absent of goodness apart from
him, though. Let's not forget to give time to acknowledging
the wonders around us, even if it feels a little like a treasure
hunt at first.

*Decide what you want to focus your attention on today and
keep bringing it back to that thought throughout the day.*

THINK ABOUT IT

Whatever is true, whatever is honorable, whatever is just, whatever is pure, whatever is lovely, whatever is commendable, if there is any excellence, if there is anything worthy of praise, think about these things.

PHILIPPIANS 4:8 ESV

This verse is full of good and practical advice. Science backs up the benefits of focusing on such things. When we focus on what is true, honorable, just, pure, pleasing, and commendable, we train our minds to look for those things and to meditate on them. As our thoughts change, so does the quality of our lives. If we are more apt to be grateful for what we have, we have higher life satisfaction.

What good news this is! It is accessible to everyone, and we don't have to buy a thing in order to put it into practice. It literally is connecting to what we already have. We simply need to focus on the life-giving aspects and joy-promoting features of this life. What do you want to think about today?

Decide the types of things you want to think about today and direct your thoughts that way.

NEVER ALONE

The LORD defends those who suffer;
he defends them in times of trouble.
Those who know the LORD trust him,
because he will not leave those who come to him.

PSALM 9:9-10 NCV

We are not alone in our sorrows or in our troubles. We have one who sees all, knows all, and is with us through whatever comes. When we go to God for help, he always hears us. He is our champion deliverer and our hope.

In our gratitude practices, it is so important to remember that we are not alone. We are part of a greater whole. Our lives may feel small, but they are not insignificant. God knows and loves us, and he cannot be convinced out of it! Let's draw near to him through prayer and a surrendered heart today. As we sense his presence and see his hand of mercy moving on our behalf, let's give him thanks.

When you feel alone, turn your attention to the presence of God. Ask him to reveal himself to you in a fresh way in this moment. Remember that the Spirit is as close as your breath, so breathe him in.

FIRST CHOICE

"You did not choose Me but I chose you, and appointed you that you would go and bear fruit, and that your fruit would remain, so that whatever you ask of the Father in My name He may give to you."

JOHN 15:16 NASB

Do you remember the days of elementary school when you would wait to be picked for a team? Perhaps you were athletic and didn't have to worry about your place in the lineup. Maybe you were picked last. No matter what your experiences of rejection or acceptance are in your life, there is one who always chooses you first.

Before we even knew to look to the Lord, he chose us as his own. We need never fear his rejection, for his love reaches us wherever we are. Let's not overlook the people who lovingly choose us as friends, partners, and family in this life. We have much to be grateful for when it comes to being the object of God's affection. At the same time, we can also honor with thankfulness those in our lives now.

Write a note of gratitude to someone important in your life and mail it to them.

THE POWER OF INTENTION

"You should go and study the meaning of the verse:
I want you to show mercy, not just offer me a sacrifice.
For I have come to invite the outcasts of society and sinners,
not those who think they are already on the right path."

MATTHEW 9:13 TPT

When we get too caught up in our actions without considering the reasoning behind them, we may lose sight of the point of it all. What is love if it is conditional? It certainly isn't the love of God. What is grace if it is only reserved for some? It isn't grace at all. We don't need to abandon our boundaries in order to put this into practice either. But we do need to be intentional.

Jesus didn't play by the rules of the religious elite of his day. He challenged them to rethink their own understanding of God's law. If Christ is our example, then we should be quick to show mercy and slow to judge. Whatever intentions we set our actions will follow. However, if we simply go through the motions but resist in our hearts, that too will be revealed.

Write down how you want others to feel when they are around you. Take intentional acts to treat them in a way that will express this.

SIGNALS OF GOD'S FAITHFULNESS

Rejoice, you people of Jerusalem!
Rejoice in the LORD your God!
For the rain he sends demonstrates his faithfulness.
Once more the autumn rains will come,
as well as the rains of spring.

JOEL 2:23 NLT

If we had no concrete relief, hope, or goodness in this life, we would struggle to believe in God at all. As it is, God has not left us without reasons to hope. He reveals his faithfulness in the world around us, and he hasn't ever stopped moving.

Science and nature are wonderful reflections of God's wisdom and care. He is creative and intentional. Instead of being overwhelmed or discouraged by circumstances, when we look for reasons to be thankful in the various difficulties in our lives, we can rejoice in what we find. Every inconvenience we encounter can be a launching point of finding new details to be grateful for and those reflect God's faithfulness.

When things don't go as expected today, look for reasons to be thankful. A missed appointment could mean more time with your family, for instance. Acknowledge the reasons you find and whisper your prayer of appreciation for each one.

BELOVED ONES

Because you are his sons,
God sent the Spirit of his Son into our hearts,
the Spirit who calls out, "Abba, Father."

GALATIANS 4:6 NIV

Gratitude can be taught as a practice. If we can learn it,
we can also encourage it in those closest to us. Consider
children and how they mirror what they see. If they see
us choosing gratitude, even in hard times, they may learn
to do the same. Aren't we all constantly learning from one
another? Let's be sure to pass on traits that benefit everyone,
at least to the best of our ability.

We are the children of God, not his slaves. We have been
adopted as his daughters and sons, and he reminds us of
who we are and in whose image we were made. The more
we mirror his goodness and generosity, the more we reflect
his likeness in our lives. What better gift of gratitude do we
have to offer him than how we choose to live?

*Pick one trait of God that you are grateful for and reflect that
in your interactions and decisions today.*

MARCH

Devote yourselves to prayer
with an alert mind
and a thankful heart.

COLOSSIANS 4:2 NLT

OPPORTUNITY TO UNDERSTAND

"The Lord does not see as man sees;
for man looks at the outward appearance,
but the Lord looks at the heart."

1 Samuel 16:7 nkjv

It can feel incredibly frustrating to be misunderstood by those close to us in our lives. We cannot assume the intentions of others, though we often do when we take offense. Still, there is one who sees the motives of our hearts, and he understands us. We can also apply grace with one another, offering others the benefit of the doubt and giving time, space, and conversation in a true effort to understanding each other. Though we cannot read each other's hearts, we can certainly try to understand where people are coming from.

Communicating about our hearts and intentions, especially when we have hurt someone with our words or actions, can make us feel incredibly vulnerable. We don't owe everyone an explanation of why we do what we do, but we should certainly take time to be understood and to also try to understand others. As an expression of gratitude for them, we can build bridges for connection rather than turning away or trying to avoid the discomfort of being vulnerable.

When someone close to you acts or speaks in a way that feels abrasive or out of character, give grace.

NEW LIFE

If anyone is in Christ, he is a new creation;
the old has passed away, and see, the new has come!

2 CORINTHIANS 5:17 CSB

There is an inherent discomfort when we go through
transitions in life. When something new is birthed, it
may be incredibly exciting, but at the same time it is a bit
disorienting. By focusing on gratitude, we can ease the hard
parts of the transition and keep our perspectives balanced.

A new job, a big move, or having a child are all life-altering
events. They feel fresh, exciting, and new, but perhaps
daunting and scary as well. Both feelings can be present at
the same time, and yet the aspects of those feelings which
we choose to focus on affect how we feel about the changes.
Consider the new changes you have already experienced
in your life, and the benefits of each. Though there may
have been some hard realities and changes in your lifestyle,
would you still choose them? As you give thought to your
gratitude for what you have already walked through, trust
that you will experience the fullness of what God has
planned for you. You can feel gratitude for the truth that
you have his help every step of the way.

*Write out a big change that is either on the horizon or has
recently happened. What are the good things that you saw
coming from it?*

INCREASED PATIENCE

Jesus Christ might display his perfect patience as an example to those who were to believe in him for eternal life.

1 TIMOTHY 1:16 ESV

Patience is one of the fruits of the Spirit. The Scriptures tell us how patient God is with humanity. As we develop greater trust in the Lord and in his faithfulness, patient endurance is a benefit we reap. When we only follow our impulses, we do not leave room for wisdom to guide us. It is always best to slow down and consider what we want to give our time, attention, and loyalty to.

Studies have shown that the practice of gratitude increases patience in people. Learning to delay gratification and prioritize what is important to us helps us to make better choices, and that in turn leads to greater satisfaction with them. Much like gratitude forces us to slow down and pay attention to the present moment, patience allows us to engage with those around us without rushing ahead and missing the important moments of life.

When you are tempted to instantly gratify an impulse, decide to make the decision later, say, in an hour, a day, or next week. Then do something with what you have right now within your grasp, especially if that means taking time to really listen to the people around you.

END THE COMPARISON

If the whole body were an eye, it would not be able to hear.
If the whole body were an ear, it would not be able to smell.
If each part of the body were the same part, there would be
no body. But truly God put all the parts, each one of them,
in the body as he wanted them.

1 CORINTHIANS 12:17-18 NCV

Comparison breeds feelings of envy, dissatisfaction, and
a misplaced urge to conform to an artificial standard.
God did not create us to compete with one another but
to support each other with our own unique gifts and
purposes. We are each a part of a larger body, and when we
act in our capacity without trying to be something that we
are not, we support each other well.

Gratitude can help us be more confident in what we have
to offer. It can help us feel more comfortable in our own
skin. Let's give up comparing our personalities, bodies, and
talents with one another. Instead, let's develop whatever
inherent qualities we do have. We are each a gift to one
another, so let's stop apologizing for what we're not and
instead be the best of who we are!

*Make a list of all the traits that you love about yourself. Ask
others who know you well if you are stumped! When you are
tempted to compare yourself to others, remind yourself of
who you are and focus on what specific work is yours to do.*

THERE'S STILL TIME

Earnestly desire the greater gifts.
And yet, I am going to show you a far better way.

1 CORINTHIANS 12:31 NASB

We are never too old to learn something new, and we need never be too stuck in old habits that we can't adopt new ones. Gratitude as a practice helps us focus on the good things in life, and that perspective helps us treat others well. No matter what talents or skills we have, we can choose to use them in a way that blesses others and does good for those in our communities.

At the same time, learning a new hobby, skill, or language humbles us and connects us to others. Now is a great time to learn that thing we've always said we wanted to learn. There are so many resources available to us today that the accessibility of learning new things is often at our fingertips. We can be grateful for what we have and still be open and intentional about doing new things.

Spend some time learning or taking steps to engage with something that you have been wanting to take up.

REASONS TO CELEBRATE

Celebrate with praises the God and Father of our Lord Jesus
Christ, who has shown us his extravagant mercy. For his
fountain of mercy has given us a new life—we are reborn to
experience a living, energetic hope through the resurrection
of Jesus Christ from the dead.

1 PETER 1:3 TPT

Finding reasons to celebrate the normal, everyday aspects
of our lives is a key element of gratitude. As we find
the mercies of God woven into the ordinary events and
occurrences, we collect treasures that lead us to becoming
someone who can easily rejoice.

Noticing the simple things that make you feel present in
your day is one way to celebrate the blessings you now have.
God has sown his goodness into the world, and we will find
the fingerprints of his mercy when we look for them. They
are all around us! An attitude of gratitude keeps us ready and
looking, so let's be sure to adopt an open perspective today.

*Take a moment to breathe a word of thanks every time you
engage with the good you find in your day.*

EVEN MORE REASON

"We are here for only a moment, visitors and strangers in the land as our ancestors were before us. Our days on earth are like a passing shadow, gone so soon without a trace."

1 CHRONICLES 29:15 NLT

Gratitude helps us connect to the present and feel more engaged in the lives we're living rather than the lives we may wish to be living. Life is too short to waste on what could have been. Every day is a gift, and we are not promised tomorrow. Considering that, we should live each day engaged in life the way we have it, aligned with our values and doing what brings us joy.

Not every part of our lives is inherently joyful. There are mundane things that just must get done. But that does not mean that we can't find reasons to give thanks for even the most menial tasks and events. A sink full of dishes needing washed can signal that we have enough food and loved ones to share it with. Let's find reasons to be grateful for even the most ordinary tasks today.

When you are dreading a task today, reframe it as a springboard for gratitude, and give thanks!

FROM THE ASHES

"He raises the poor from the dust
and lifts the needy from the ash heap;
he seats them with princes
and has them inherit a throne of honor."

1 SAMUEL 2:8 NIV

There will be times in this life when we are face down in the dirt. We may be sitting in the ashes of broken dreams. Even in these barren places, God's love reaches us. We are not destitute or without hope. Our God lifts us from the dust and the ash heap and puts us in places of honor in his kingdom. He redeems us, restores us, and never holds our weaknesses against us. What a wonderful God he is!

When we feel beaten down by life, let's not forget that we have a Savior who comes to our help. We are not too far from his mercy, for his mercies reach us no matter where we are. Even if it is a struggle to hope for new life, we can trust that the morning will come and with it the light of a new day!

Remember a time when you felt as if you had lost it all and what came from that time. As you give thanks for living through that time, name what you are thankful for which came out of it.

LOVE'S LIGHT

He has delivered us from the power of darkness and
conveyed us into the kingdom of the Son of His love.

COLOSSIANS 1:13 NKJV

Love is expansive and freeing. It does not seek to control.
Love's light shines on each of us, just as the sun's rays reach
everyone in its path. God's love is not discriminatory or
exclusive. It is offered to everyone in the same unending
measure. Each of us can warm ourselves in the light of
God's love, coming alive as we turn our faces to him.

How has love affected the way you live, move, and relate to
others? There is no darkness that the smallest flame cannot
light up. What if you thought of each moment of gratitude
as a match being struck to shine the light in goodness? If
you were to light a few each day, you would soon find that
there is more goodness to find hidden in the shadows of
your life than you could have imagined.

*Take a walk and observe the beauty around you. As you
acknowledge each specific form you find, thank God that
there are also details of beauty in your own life.*

GRATEFUL FOR THE HELP

Since he himself has suffered when he was tempted,
he is able to help those who are tempted.

HEBREWS 2:18 CSB

When we are going through a tough time, it can be hard to find solace in the company or advice of people who don't understand. It is not to say that their support means nothing, but there is a special kind of solidarity in one who knows what you are going through because they themselves have been through it. There is deep compassion that goes beyond words. What a comfort this can be to our souls.

Christ lived the human experience. He knows what it is to go hungry and to be overtired and overworked. He knows what temptation feels like. He knows! Let's lean on his help, then, and be grateful that he doesn't just tell us what is good for us—he has lived it.

Mental subtraction is a practice that can help you be grateful for what you have by imagining its absence. Try this while you are doing something rather mindless today, perhaps while you are taking a shower, washing the dishes, or going for a walk. Imagine what your day would be like without hot water, serviceable plates and cups, or even legs that work so hard for you.

THE GOOD STUFF

He has told you, O man, what is good,
and what does the LORD require of you.
But to do justice, and to love kindness,
and to walk humbly with your God?

MICAH 6:8 ESV

This verse is so simple yet so explicit at the same time. What is good in the eyes of the Lord? The verse in Micah tells us to do justice, to love kindness, and to walk humbly with him. Studies also support the benefits of standing for what is right, choosing kindness, and being humble. A gratitude practice can help make these choices a bit more natural.

The more you look for the good in your life, the more prone you will be to see it. As you look for the positives, you will also more clearly see the barriers that stand against accomplishing those goals. Standing for justice on behalf of the oppressed is a way that we can actively engage with gratitude for the freedom we have. Let's choose kindness and keep an open heart, for these are good standards to live by!

Look for ways to do the good that God has called us to in his Word. When you see injustices, take a stand. Be kind to everyone. Walk humbly and be willing to learn new things as you admit to what you don't know.

THE PATH TO FREEDOM

He gave himself for us so he might pay the price to free us from all evil and to make us pure people who belong only to him—people who are always wanting to do good deeds.

TITUS 2:14 NCV

Gratitude helps us to see the value in the people around us. When we are focused on others' faults, we will diminish whatever positives they have to offer and perhaps even miss the gift of who they are as a friend and a member of the community. When we focus on reasons to be thankful for the people in our lives, we strengthen the bonds between us with the glue of gratitude.

Gratitude frees us from the negative cycles we may find ourselves in. Especially in an age when most news is bad news and there's no shortage of it, we must fight fear by grounding ourselves in the goodness of God. There are reasons for joy all around us and practicing gratitude trains us to see it. What freedom there is in knowing that there is such beauty in the lives we currently live!

For every person you encounter today, think of one thing about them that you see as a gift. Maybe it's their unique perspective or their gracious smile. Acknowledge this quality and keep going. You may find that you enjoy people more as you do!

HEART POSTURE

The Spirit also helps our weakness; for we do not know
what to pray for as we should, but the Spirit Himself
intercedes for us with groanings too deep for words.

ROMANS 8:26 NASB

We don't have to have the words to express our gratitude
in order to properly embrace it. The practice of noticing
is a form of mindfulness. We can overthink our practices
by needing them to look a certain way all the time. There
are moments when words fail us, and that's okay. In those
moments, let's allow what is moving us to do so.

In times when we don't know what to say or do, God's Spirit
helps us. God doesn't need our put-together speeches to
know what is on our hearts. Perhaps we can let our practice
of gratitude become a bit abstract when we find ourselves at
a loss. With open hearts, we can trust the Lord to see what is
there inside of us, even if we don't know how to express it.

*Instead of using words to express gratitude today, do
something more abstract yet still expressive. Dance, paint,
play a tune, or do whatever form it takes, and let it be what
it is without overthinking it.*

WHAT WE NEED

To the fatherless he is a father.
To the widow he is a champion friend.
The lonely he makes part of a family.
The prisoners he leads into prosperity
until they sing for joy.
This is our Holy God in his Holy Place!

PSALM 68:5-6 TPT

Though no one is perfect, and no one has the perfect life, God fills our unmet needs with the abundance of who he is. He is an attentive and tender Father. He is a close friend, always there when we need him. He sets us in his family, no matter how lonely we feel. There is so much to be grateful for in the wonderful provisions of God.

We experience grief in this world, and God does not demand otherwise. He is a Comforter to the broken-hearted; he is wisdom to those who are confused. He is present in the fullness of his perfect love. When we see our need today, let's remember that it is an invitation to know God as our sustenance and breakthrough. He meets us in it!

When you are presented with a need or a void in your life today, bring it to God and ask him to meet you in all the fullness of who he is.

CONFIDENT STEPS

Seek his will in all you do,
and he will show you which path to take.

PROVERBS 3:6 NLT

Mindful decisions lead to greater confidence. We can only take steps based on the information we have. We should choose according to what aligns with God's kingdom and with our own gifts. No one else can make the decision for us. Even if there is great pressure from outside sources to do something or take a certain path, we should weigh those decisions and make them from a place of ownership over them.

There is so much grace as we journey through this life. We may make our plans, but only God knows how it will play out. Let's trust him to guide us into his goodness every step of the way. As we follow the path of his love, he uncovers each next step and when necessary, he redirects us. We can trust him because he is faithful. There is even freedom to try and fail. With wisdom as our guide, we are never alone.

With big and little choices today, take time to think through them before you give your yes or no.

WONDERFUL THINGS

LORD, you are my God;
I will exalt you and praise your name,
for in perfect faithfulness
you have done wonderful things,
things planned long ago.

ISAIAH 25:1 NIV

Our hearts grow in appreciation and awe as we recount the things that God has done for us! When we take time to remember what we've walked through already in both devastating and wonderful experiences, we can offer gratitude to God for his help. He gave us his own resilience as he brought us through it all.

Take time to remember some of the wonderful moments you have experienced. Go through the highlight reel of your life and let that goodness wash over you. Many of the best moments of our lives occur after tough times. Perhaps the contrast between the lows and highs makes the successes feel even more wonderful. In any case, the Lord is faithful to us. There is no ending that is not also a new beginning, and his mercies are new every day!

As you remember the wonderful times of your life, don't forget to include the reality of what you are living now which felt like a dream in the past.

EYES FIXED

"Do not turn aside; for then you would go after empty things which cannot profit or deliver, for they are nothing."

1 SAMUEL 12:21 NKJV

It is easy to get distracted by tasks that keep our days busy but take us off course from what truly matters. If we are not careful, we may find that we are chasing empty time consumers that don't add to the value of our lives. Gratitude and intentionality go together. When we regularly evaluate how we are spending our time as well as what is most important to us in the season we are in, we can make the necessary adjustments.

There are many things in this world that keep us from experiencing satisfaction in our lives. Consumerism keeps us insatiably wanting the next thing. Our jobs sometimes demand more from us than we can give in a forty-hour workweek. However, if we keep our eyes fixed on what is important, we can be more intentional about keeping our boundaries in place.

Before you jump into a list of to-dos today, prioritize the most important tasks and ensure that they are aligned with your values. Let go of what cannot and need not be done today.

THE IMPORTANCE OF VISION

"I will pour out my Spirit on all humanity;
then your sons and your daughters will prophesy,
your old men will have dreams,
and your young men will see visions."

JOEL 2:28 CSB

No matter how young or old we are, perspective is always important. Though our understanding may feel set, we are constantly learning and taking in information. None of us knows it all—not even close! Not even experts know all there is to know about their area of expertise. As we take on the posture of lifelong learners, we can more readily take on new information as we discover what we didn't know before.

Imagination is an important part of our ability to grow. Innovation comes through creative breakthroughs, not by remaining stagnant in old forms that no longer serve us well. Can we partner with the innovative spirit of creation that God's Spirit offers us by dreaming bigger and envisioning what we have not yet experienced? Gratitude connects us to the present, and it can also make us more aware of the possibilities of tomorrow.

After spending a few minutes being grateful for what you have, take a few more to envision what you can do with it.

ROOTED IN TRUST

"You keep him in perfect peace
whose mind is stayed on you,
because he trusts in you."

ISAIAH 26:3 ESV

Consistency builds trust. As we walk with the Lord and he proves his faithfulness to us, our trust in him grows. The perfect peace of God's presence is like an anchor for our souls. It keeps us in place so we will not be tossed to and fro by the waves of fear. When we have solid anchor points to which we can connect our faith, we remain rooted in trust.

Gratitude can clarify these points in our lives. Where there is steady peace and practical stability, there also are grounds for gratitude. Look for the places, people, and things that are consistent, life-giving, and true. You can trust that the one who gives good gifts will continue to take care of you.

Consider the steadiest people and routines in your life and give thanks for each of them. Reach out to the people whom you depend on and thank them for their loyalty, love, and support.

OUTSIDE OF US

If we are not faithful, he will still be faithful,
because he must be true to who he is.

2 TIMOTHY 2:13 NCV

God's faithfulness is not dependent on our own. That is extraordinarily good news. We don't have to worry about God putting contingencies on his promises. He is as faithful in love on our worst days as he is on our best.

It can be incredibly encouraging to look for the gifts of life that have nothing to do with what we have to offer. The sun is not dictated by our behavior, and neither is the rain. There is air to breathe and a landing place to lay our heads no matter what we do or don't accomplish. Though we may find satisfaction in our work, we must be careful to not let our worth get wrapped up in what we produce. We are worthy of love because we are made in the image of the Creator. Every human is deserving of care, comfort, and rest. Let's not count ourselves above, beneath, or outside of this truth!

Meditate on the basics of this life which you don't need to work for to enjoy. Spend at least a few minutes giving thanks for them.

THE POWER OF PRACTICE

The kingdom of God is not in words, but in power.

1 CORINTHIANS 4:20 NASB

We all know people who talk a good talk but don't follow through on what they say. Words are meaningless without the proper action behind them. This is as true in our personal practices as it is in our relationships. If we want to build a habit of gratitude, then we must follow through with the practice of it for more than a day.

We don't have to work out for an hour each day to see the benefits of exercise. We don't have to dedicate an entire day each week to spending time with our friends to deepen our relationships. In the same way, a little investment into thinking about our blessings can really go a long way. We build momentum over time, but it is in the consistency of our practices that allows us to see results. If we want gratitude to change our perspectives over time, then we must be proactive with it. With that in mind, let's make meaningful changes with manageable steps that can be done every day.

I you haven't done so already, plan in the next month to add a practice of gratitude to each day. Be specific and keep it manageable. Try working it in before you go to sleep, for instance. Start with listing three things about your day that you are grateful for.

SO MUCH MORE

This is why the Scriptures say:
Things never discovered or heard of before,
things beyond our ability to imagine—
these are the many things God has in store
for all his lovers.

1 CORINTHIANS 2:9 TPT

The kingdom of God is one of abundance, not of scarcity. If you look for good things in your life, you will find them. We all have things to be grateful for, and what's more, every day is a new opportunity to find fresh reasons. Every day is a new slate, and every moment is its own gift. There is more goodness in God's plans than we can ever imagine. Why shouldn't we engage with this goodness with a sense of joy and wonder?

If you have been keeping a record of the things you are grateful for, take some time to go through them today. What a treasure trove of goodness there is around you. Now engage with the beauty of your life today; allow yourself to hope for what you will find tomorrow. Remain open with a sense of awe and thank God for all that he has yet to reveal to you.

As you take in all that God has already given you, thank him for the things you can't even imagine that he has in store for you yet.

THE TREASURE OF CONTENTMENT

True godliness with contentment is itself great wealth.

1 TIMOTHY 6:6 NLT

We don't have to wait for our lives to change before we experience contentment. We can cultivate it through gratitude. The verses following 1 Timothy 6:6 say, "After all, we brought nothing with us when we came into the world, and we can't take anything with us when we leave it. So, if we have enough food and clothing, let us be content" (vv 7-8).

When we recognize that our basic needs are taken care of, we can rest in that knowledge. We have enough, and in fact many of us have more than enough. Instead of focusing on what we don't have, when we focus on what we do have, we garner a greater peace with our lives as they are. That peace may lead to better sleep, a more positive outlook, and boosted energy levels. Truly, the benefits are worth putting thankfulness into practice.

Whenever you find yourself worried about something out of your control or you feel the tug of dissatisfaction with your life, consider whether your basic needs are being met and focus on what you do have.

COMFORTING COMPASSION

Praise be to the God and Father of our Lord Jesus Christ,
the Father of compassion and the God of all comfort.

2 CORINTHIANS 1:3 NIV

There are some emotions that bind us to others. Gratitude
and compassion are two of them. Gratitude may ground
us in the goodness present in our own lives, but it also
strengthens our relationships with others. Gratitude is not
just about what we have or what is enough for us, it gives us
an enhanced perspective.

Compassion offers grace instead of criticism. It gives space
to the experience of another without any demands. How
many of us have needed a listening ear and instead got
a lecture? When we lead with compassion, we choose to
listen and comfort, but we don't have to fix what is not
asking to be fixed. Let's give gratitude for the comfort we've
received through compassion and choose to move in the
same spirit.

*Today, listen to a friend who needs to talk something out.
Instead of jumping in with advice, offer them the time and
space to speak, and respond with compassion and comfort
when it is appropriate.*

WONDERS OF REVELATION

"He reveals deep and secret things;
He knows what is in the darkness,
And light dwells with Him."

DANIEL 2:22 NKJV

When we take time to be grateful for what we have, we make room for discovering new things. God is a wise teacher, and the Holy Spirit loves to reveal the deep insights of his heart to those who take the time to listen.

The presence of God is accessible at any and every moment. We only need to slow down and focus on his nearness. Gratitude works in the same way. When we turn our attention to what is true and good, our eyes are opened to the wonders that are already around us. The light of God is here, and we can find it by practicing an astute presence of mind and tuning into his Spirit. There are wonders galore in his wisdom, and we will not miss what he is speaking when we take time to listen for his voice.

Pray and ask the Lord to open your ears to his voice. As you go about your day, turn your focus to the goodness of God as you encounter it.

WORTH WAITING

From ancient times no one has heard,
no one has listened to,
no eye has seen any God except you
who acts on behalf of the one who waits for him.

ISAIAH 64:4 CSB

In the waiting periods of life, we can be tempted to lose hope. One of the greatest tools we have for endurance is gratitude. When we recognize what we should be thankful for today, our hearts have reasons to hope that we will find even more goodness tomorrow. When we try to rush ahead, we may miss out on the beauty and lessons we have yet to discover along the slower path.

In our youth, we all seem to be in a rush to get from point A to point B. As we grow older and experience the detours of life, most of us realize that we cannot control time, and really, there is no need to try. When we learn to embrace our lives for what they are rather than wistfully wish them away because of what they aren't, we can more readily accept the gifts that are here now as we wait for what is yet to be.

When you feel the need today to rush, choose instead to slow down so you can engage fully with what you are doing.

A SAFE PLACE

"All that the Father gives me will come to me,
and whoever comes to me I will never cast out."

JOHN 6:37 ESV

When we come to the Lord, he accepts us as his own. He lovingly tends to us as we yield our hearts and lives to him. Even when we fail or fall, his love keeps us close. We cannot convince Christ away from his mercy toward us, so let's not count ourselves out.

This world is full of fickle fancies that change as often as the winds shift. There are some things that we simply cannot count on for longevity. That does not mean that they can't be appreciated for what they are in the moment. Even so, there is a love that will never leave us, even on our darkest days. We will not be cast out of the kingdom of God for making mistakes; he does not require our perfection. He is a safe place to try and fail and try again. Hallelujah!

Just because something doesn't last forever doesn't mean it is meaningless. Look for ways you can be grateful for your temporary blessings and remember that God's love is forever.

AUDIENCE OF ONE

"Your Father, whom you cannot see, will see you.
Your Father sees what is done in secret,
and he will reward you."

MATTHEW 6:18 NCV

If we are not careful, we can be convinced into thinking that the things of this life that no one else sees or notices are not worthy. We are allowed to enjoy things simply for the pleasure of them without looking for ways to make an impact with them. Some things can be a simple hobby rather than a side hustle or ministry. God delights in the things we delight in, and he does not always demand that we use them in a way that earns a living or kingdom points.

When we are rooted in the love of God and his knowledge of us, we don't have to feel any pressure to perform for others. What is done in secret is as valued by God as what is done for everyone to see. Let your personal joy be what it is, and delight in it because it connects you to God and to your own creativity.

Work on something that makes you happy today, whether it is a project, music, or exercise. Allow it to be just for your own joy without sharing it with others.

WORK IN PROGRESS

I am confident of this very thing, that He who began a good work among you will complete it by the day of Christ Jesus.

PHILIPPIANS 1:6 NASB

We are all works in progress. Even those whom we think have it all are still in progress. Don't be fooled into thinking you are behind in life. That kind of thinking only burdens us into comparisons, but you are on a unique journey in this life. Quit comparing so you can fall in love with where you're at today. It is possible!

Even recognizing that you are in progress—that no one has completed the voyage through life until they are in their last moments—can take the pressure off. You have not experienced all the good that you will in this life, and there is still more ahead of you. Even so, dig into the beauty that is already yours as a reminder that life is worth engaging in and you are on a uniquely wonderful journey that is all your own.

Visually map what you are grateful for through a collage, a few pictures, or a list. Put your creation where you can look at it and be reminded of the myriad of things for which you can be thankful.

FEARLESS CONFIDENCE

The one who walks in integrity
will experience a fearless confidence in life,
but the one who is devious
will eventually be exposed.

PROVERBS 10:9 TPT

When we live according to our values, we have no reason to try to escape our lives. With integrity infused into our daily choices, we have nothing to fear. We can walk confidently knowing that though we are not perfect, we are doing our best to live honestly and humbly before the Lord and others.

In order to live aligned to the values of Christ's kingdom, we must first know what they are. There are many, but a good place to start is in the verses outlining the fruits of the Spirit. Do we already live by some of these behaviors; do we need to grow and be more intentional about others of these qualities? Living with integrity is a decision to be the same person no matter whom we are around. Let's stop shapeshifting to suit the people we hang with, and instead let's be true to who we are and who we want to be.

Which traits of God mean the most to you? In recognizing these, we often find the values with which we most align. As an act of gratitude, plan practical ways to incorporate these traits into your interactions with people today.

BENEFITS IN SUFFERING

My suffering was good for me,
for it taught me to pay attention to your decrees.

PSALM 119:71 NLT

Nobody likes to suffer. It's not a pleasant part of life, but a necessary one, nonetheless. None of us can escape the suffering of sorrow, grief, or loss. We cannot control how it will show up in our lives, we just know that it will. Does this mean we should live in fear? By no means! Should we assume that our suffering is a punishment? Not at all.

Whatever ways in which we suffer, we can be sure of this: God is with us in it. He does not leave us destitute or without comfort. Even when our lives feel as if they are being ripped apart at the seams, we still have air to breathe, food to eat, and people who care for us and whom we can lean on. Though our gratitude does not eliminate our suffering, it can diminish the negative effects of it. By turning our attention to what remains true, good, and hopeful, we can increase our resilience. Let's not ignore this powerful tool that helps shift our perspective from negative to positive.

When you are faced with suffering, make sure you take time to practice naming the good that still endures. Though it may not change your circumstances, over time it can change your perspective and bring relief.

APRIL

Praise the LORD.
Give thanks to the LORD,
for he is good;
his love endures forever.

PSALM 106:1 NIV

ALL ABOUT LOVE

Many waters cannot quench love;
rivers cannot sweep it away.
If one were to give
all the wealth of one's house for love,
it would be utterly scorned.

SONG OF SOLOMON 8:7 NIV

The love of God cannot be overstated. Ephesians 3 puts it this way: "I pray that you…may have power…to grasp how wide and long and high and deep is the love of Christ, and to know this love that surpasses knowledge" (vv 17-19). The love of God is likened to the fullness of God. When we receive his love, we receive him.

There are multiple expressions of love. We give and receive love in different ways. We form ideals around it, and yet we can never reach the end of God's limitless love. It is far grander than what we can put words to, and still more powerful than we've experienced. What fullness we find in fellowship with the one who is love. May we not take for granted the incredible power of love that is available to us today!

Give thanks for the love you have in your life from your pets, your friends, your family, your parents, and God himself.

PEACE IN THE UNKNOWN

A man's heart plans his way,
But the LORD directs his steps.

PROVERBS 16:9 NKJV

Oh, the plans we make for our lives. The older we get, the more readily we recognize that though we may plan our path, there are often obstacles that redirect us. We can't anticipate what we can't see, but God is never thrown off. When our plans are derailed, God's aren't. We can trust that even in midst of the great unknowns, the Lord directs our steps. If we're honest with ourselves, it is all unknown to us anyway.

Does the unknown excite or terrify you? Perhaps it's both or it could be neither. Whatever the unknown evokes in you, you can trust that God sees all, leads you in love, and has grace enough to cover your missteps. He doesn't care about perfection, so you can lay that down. Lean on his presence, for he will guide you in wisdom every step of the way.

Consider some worries you have had in the past that ended up not coming to pass. Write down the provision that occurred instead, and trust that what God did then he can do again and again for you.

MULTIPLIED EFFORTS

The one who provides seed for the sower and bread for food will also provide and multiply your seed and increase the harvest of your righteousness.

2 CORINTHIANS 9:10 CSB

As is often the case, when you join your intentions to your practices, the return you receive can be greatly multiplied. If your practices are partnered with wisdom and hard work, it will be even better. Building a practice of gratitude is more than just saying you will be more grateful. It requires work in turning our attention to our lives and homing in on the smallest of details. The more we do it, the more natural it becomes. This isn't just a hopeful wish, but a studied and proven result.

Though the beginning of your growth in gratitude may seem small, trust that as you put your efforts into practice, the results will speak for themselves. God provides seed for the sower, and he has planted goodness in your life. He has already provided all that you have to be grateful for today. Trust that he who started this work will continue to bless it as you put in the work!

Think back to a time when you had a small start in some growth project, and it grew into something bigger than you could have imagined. Take each day and turn your attention to the goodness in it.

KEEP ENCOURAGING

Encourage one another and build one another up,
just as you are doing.

1 THESSALONIANS 5:11 ESV

Our relationships don't deepen by accident. With intentional connection we become close to others. It is natural that over time we may relax into roles that feel comfortable, but for many of us that means we become less intentional with our encouragement. The importance of appreciation goes beyond our personal practices to the strength of our relationships.

Gratitude has been shown to strengthen our social bonds. As with all personal qualities, this takes consistency in how you put it into practice. Just giving a single word of encouragement and then moving on with our lives is not a relationship builder. However, if we put our intentions and practices together, we can build habits that remind us to include encouragement consistently. As we do, our bonds with others will strengthen, especially if that encouragement is genuine. People like to feel seen and appreciated; taking the time to thank someone for what they have done and who they are benefits both the giver and the receiver.

Look for at least one specific, genuine thought to encourage each person you meet today.

INNER WORK

With God's power working in us, God can do much,
much more than anything we can ask or imagine.

EPHESIANS 3:20 NCV

The power of God transforms us from the inside out. The
same is true with the practice of gratitude! It starts in our
inner worlds—the space shared by our thoughts and our
feelings—and as we choose gratitude more and more, our
lives become motivated by it.

Psalm 100:4 says, "Come into his city with songs of
thanksgiving and into his courtyards with songs of praise.
Thank him and praise his name." We enter his courts
through fellowship with his Spirit. We don't have to
physically go anywhere; it is a journey our hearts make.
What joy we find as we come with thankful hearts before
the throne of our Father. What joy we, too, can find as we
begin each day with gratitude for the lives we have!

*Building a habit takes intention and discipline. Creating a
space for gratitude in our lives means practicing it. Evaluate
which practices of gratitude have felt easier and which have
felt more challenging. Adjust your practice to what naturally
works for you and make that time—morning, noon, or
night—set firmly in your schedule.*

LIVING AND ACTIVE

The word of God is living and active, and sharper than any
two-edged sword, even penetrating as far as the division of
soul and spirit, of both joints and marrow, and able to judge
the thoughts and intentions of the heart.

HEBREWS 4:12 NASB

In the first chapter of John, Jesus is called the Word of God.
He is the living Word, the one who still speaks and whose
voice reverberates throughout all of creation. The wisdom
of his truth is sharp and clear. Looking at the ministry of
Jesus and what he stated repeatedly, it is the law of his love
that flies like a banner over every one of his teachings.

When we choose to align ourselves in the love of God, we
have no excuses if we deride anyone including ourselves.
His love unifies and builds up; it does not seek to destroy
people. We can stand on the living Word of God if we
humble ourselves as his servants in the sight of men. If that
feels hard, that's because it is. It is by grace and grace alone
that we can choose this path. But a practice of gratitude
helps us outweigh the hard truths with the benefits of grace.
We are lavishly loved, so it's with this same measure that we
can act in the Spirit toward others.

*Instead of asserting your opinions over those you disagree
with, focus on what you can agree on.*

OVERFLOWING COMPASSION

"Overflow with mercy and compassion for others,
just as your heavenly Father overflows
with mercy and compassion for all."

LUKE 6:36 TPT

We can give from a place of overflow when we are already ourselves filled. The Scriptures say that God overflows with mercy and compassion for all, not for a few. His resources are endless, and his nature is abundant. We don't have to beg him for something that he already offers us freely!

Getting in touch with gratitude opens us to what already exists in our lives. There is mercy and compassion present in many forms. And still, we can receive fresh portions today. When we are running low on patience, grace, and kindness, there is more we can fill up on if we seek the presence of God. As we are attuned to the abundance of Christ's love in our lives, we can give to others in the same way. As an act of gratitude, we can offer the same kindnesses that we receive. Love is not limited, so let's not limit our expressions of it.

Volunteer to help with a cause that is close to your heart.

TAKE A BREAK

The apostles returned to Jesus from their ministry tour and told him all they had done and taught. Then Jesus said, "Let's go off by ourselves to a quiet place and rest awhile." He said this because there were so many people coming and going that Jesus and his apostles didn't even have time to eat.

MARK 6:30-31 NLT

Our world never truly shuts down. It is hard to take time off from constantly being a consumer. We need physical rest, and we need emotional rest. When we are always bombarded by propaganda and messages promoting a product or a perceived need, we can eventually be worn down by it. Perhaps we even feel a bit disconnected from ourselves.

We all know to take the necessary time to rest after a big event, but many of us overlook the mental and emotional rest we may need as a regular occurrence every day. When our lives are demanding, we don't do ourselves any favors by constantly feeding on media. When we leave our minds and hearts room to breathe without listening to media mentality, we can connect with ourselves and be grateful for who we are.

As you take some time for yourself and disconnect from distractions, write down ten things that you are thankful for and love about yourself. This can lead to higher self-esteem.

SWEET SLEEP

When you lie down, you will not be afraid;
when you lie down, your sleep will be sweet.

PROVERBS 3:24 NIV

There are more than psychological and emotional benefits to gratitude. There are also physical ones. One of the reported benefits is that gratitude leads to better sleep. For those who often ruminate at night, sleep can be elusive. The negativity cycle can go into overdrive. In studies of those who practice gratitude right before going to bed, however, it has been proven that they sleep better. Who doesn't want a better night of slumber?

Regularly incorporating gratitude into your life at bedtime helps you focus on the positive thoughts and aspects of your life. It can keep the negative self-talk away which so often happens at bedtime. Consider, then, doing yourself a favor and commit to focusing on your reasons to be thankful before you drift off to sleep.

Before you go to bed each night this week, think through your day and find at least three things that you are thankful for. They can be small or big, simple, or complex.

TIED TO HOPE

"Return to the stronghold,
You prisoners of hope.
Even today I declare
That I will restore double to you."

ZECHARIAH 9:12 NKJV

When we lose hope, it can be disorienting. We may feel as if we are floating in the unknown. Instead of feeling positive about our lives, we may feel discouraged or depressed. Though gratitude is not a cure for depression, it can help us root to the good things that are still available in our lives. It may help us bring back the hope we have in other areas of our lives.

God is not finished with you yet, and he is incredibly good, trustworthy, and kind. He has more than enough to fill your life with goodness and your heart with hope. He does not lie, and he does not withhold from those who look to him for help. He is abundant in mercy, overflowing in grace, and always ready to restore more to you than you lost.

Consider the role that hope has played in your life. How does gratitude connect you back to hope? Reframe past events through the lens of gratitude and see how that might shift your perspective.

OPEN YOUR EARS

"I stand at the door and knock.
If anyone hears my voice and opens the door,
I will come in to him and eat with him, and he with me."

REVELATION 3:20 CSB

There are small invitations in our everyday lives—invitations to slow down, enjoy the people around us, and engage with those who try to connect with us. Jesus himself stands at the door of our hearts and knocks. He is always ready to fellowship with us. As we ground ourselves in the moment, we can more readily pick up the cues that are vying for our attention.

One way to become more attuned to the present and to what is happening around us is by purposefully paying attention. Gratitude helps us pay attention by directing our focus toward what in our surroundings to be thankful for. As we look for reasons to be grateful, we are more readily able to see what we might have missed otherwise.

Spend time outside today and tune into the sounds around you. Listen for specific sounds and what they represent. Notice how paying attention makes you feel in the moment.

SPRING'S JOYS

"The flowers appear on the earth,
the time of singing has come,
and the voice of the turtledove
is heard in our land."

SONG OF SOLOMON 2:12 ESV

In the transition from winter's cold, barren grip to spring's renewal and lengthening days, there is much to be thankful for. We can be grateful that warmer days are upon us. Every day we can watch the leaves grow and the flowers peek up from the ground. Overnight it seems as though each day brings more growth all around us. It is an exciting and hopeful time.

Gratitude helps bring our attention to the good things happening around us, and the more we practice it, the more goodness we see. Spend today looking for beauty in the natural world. You can be even more specific, and look for certain flowers, trees, or animals. As you pay attention to these natural beauties, your consciousness will be drawn to them. What a powerful tool this is for balancing the negatives we so often encounter. Power your attention with intention and rejoice in the evidence of spring's joys all around you.

At the end of the day, reflect on how this practice of looking for beauty in nature was for you.

COMPLETELY FILLED

"I am a God who is near," says the LORD.
"I am also a God who is far away.
No one can hide
where I cannot see him," says the LORD.
"I fill all of heaven and earth."

JEREMIAH 23:23-24 NCV

The earth is filled with the glory of God. There is not a place we can go where we can escape from his presence. This is an incredible truth that opens us up to the possibilities of goodness no matter where we roam or what we go through.

God is near, and God is also far away. There are many truths in the Scriptures like this: two opposites that remain true at the same time. If we are prone to binary thinking, this can be a tough idea to grasp, and yet there is so much more at work in the world than the two extremes of a spectrum. God is near, God is far away, and God is everywhere. Can we be open to finding him in the most unexpected places?

When you are caught in a position with no wiggle room, and you have a rigid need to resist other points of view, breathe out the need to control the narrative. Thank God that he sees and knows what you cannot. Be open to seeing alternative perspectives that resonate with his truth and love. You may find him where you did not know he was.

NOTHING IS TOO SMALL

"Are five sparrows not sold for two assaria? And yet not one
of them has gone unnoticed in the sight of God."

LUKE 12:6 NASB

No small detail is too insignificant to not cherish. God sees
the sparrows of the air, the worms of the earth, and every
living thing in all of creation. Not one goes unnoticed.
How much more, then, does he notice and take care of us?
We can be like the Lord today by taking notice of the little
things and engaging with the larger world around us.

Gratitude may start as an inner practice, but it leads to us
connecting with what is outside of us as well. Whether it is
the natural world, the people around us, or the cities we live
in, there is so much to engage us in the beautiful details. As
we take stock today, we can remain open to the wonder and
awe of the intricacies of how things fit into a larger tapestry.
This includes each one of us!

*Pay attention to the little things that capture your attention
today. Tale notice of as many as you can throughout the day.*

PEACE OF HEART

God is your confidence in times of crisis,
keeping your heart at rest in every situation.

PROVERBS 3:26 TPT

The peace of God is not a passing thing. You can rest in it through every trial and storm. It is available in times of crisis as well as in times of calm. Don't let your circumstances dictate how worried or anxious you are. When you feel this way, come to the Lord, give him all your cares; name them one by one, and leave them with him. As you do, turn your attention to that which remains unchanged and good.

Do you have enough food? Do you have a roof over your head? Do you have the support of loved ones? Be specific to your own situation, and don't forget that God is your confidence in times of trouble. He never changes, and he's never surprised. He is loyal in love and faithful to his promises. He will not leave you—no, not ever!

Take a picture of everything you encounter that you are grateful for in the moment. At the end of the day or the week, look over those precious images.

TRANSFORMED THINKING

Don't copy the behavior and customs of this world, but let God transform you into a new person by changing the way you think. Then you will learn to know God's will for you, which is good and pleasing and perfect.

ROMANS 12:2 NLT

Scripture points out how powerful our thinking is. Those who are transformed by the values of God's kingdom see the world through a different lens. We don't have to copy the customs of this world when there is refreshing wisdom that offers freedom, new life, and mercy. The behavior of those of this world may be focused on self-preservation, but the behavior of the people in God's kingdom seeks to serve others and bring redemption instead of chaos and control.

Studies show that building a habit of gratitude can train your mind to look for the positives around you. Paying attention to the little things that are good, beautiful, and beneficial can rewire your brain to look for more. As you practice being grateful, you will be transformed by it.

Decide the things you want to focus your attention on today. Bring your mind back to them throughout the day. Thank God that your mind is not so made up that you cannot see things from a transformed perspective.

WISDOM AND STRENGTH

The foolishness of God is wiser than human wisdom,
and the weakness of God is stronger than human strength.

1 CORINTHIANS 1:25 NIV

Jesus Christ is the wisdom of God personified. He embodies the strength of God, evident throughout his life on earth and in the sacrifice he made at the end of it. Psalm 20:7 says, "Some trust in chariots and some in horses, but we trust in the name of the Lord our God." The power of God is more than displays of amazing strength. It meets with us through the mercy of Christ and the power of the Holy Spirit.

Wisdom and strength are available through Christ today. Fellowship with the Spirit offers us insight into truth and empowers us to choose the values of God's kingdom. Gratitude connects us with the present, and so does fellowshipping with the King of kings and Lord of lords.

Spend ten minutes or more in prayer today thanking God for all you have and asking for his help to make wise choices. Focus your attention on his nearness and breathe in the peace of his presence for you will find strength there.

PAYING ATTENTION

Your ears shall hear a word behind you, saying,
"This is the way, walk in it,"
Whenever you turn to the right hand
Or whenever you turn to the left."

ISAIAH 30:21 NKJV

When we are distracted, it can be hard to focus on what is right in front of us. This goes for our relationships as well as our responsibilities. If we're not careful, our minds can travel far from our lives as they truly are. This may weaken our relationship to the present; it can affect the strength of our bonds, our satisfaction with daily life, and the ability to make decisions that align with our values.

When we are mindfully engaged with the present, we can be more intentional with our interactions and choices. Gratitude is a key element that keeps us connected to the lives we are already living. It helps us pay attention, which in turn helps us to hear God's voice and see his hand in our lives.

When your mind starts to wander too far into the fearful future or to venture into dark moments in the past, bring yourself back to the moment by finding specific things around you for which you are grateful.

ANCIENT WISDOM

Whatever was written in the past was written for our instruction, so that we may have hope through endurance and through the encouragement from the Scriptures.

ROMANS 15:4 CSB

The wisdom of Scripture is being backed up by science. Gratitude, for instance, is a theme throughout the Bible. Giving thanks, encouraging each other, connecting with the presence of the Lord—these are all seen throughout the Word of God. Studies show that gratitude is good for our physical, psychological, and emotional wellness.

We may not know all the reasons behind God's wisdom, but we can trust that he is good and what he asks of us is good for us. He knows what lies beneath the surface even when we don't. Time will tell of the treasures found in the Word and of following his ways.

Spend some time in prayer thanking God for what he's done for you. List the characteristics you love about him. Let it draw you closer to his heart and deeper into trust.

COMPELLED TO SERVE

"Who is the greater, one who reclines at table or one who serves? Is it not the one who reclines at table? But I am among you as the one who serves."

LUKE 22:27 ESV

Jesus led by example. He knew that his identity was the way to reveal to us what the Father is truly like. If we want to be like him, we will seek opportunities to serve others. Pride is a trap, but a humble heart keeps us open to love in all its forms.

The best leaders are those who serve alongside those they lead. They aren't afraid of hard work. May we recognize these leaders when they are in our lives and honor them with our gratitude. Let's work to be these kinds of leaders ourselves. Studies show that gratitude can connect us to others and compel us to give back.

Go out of your way to serve someone today without asking for anything in return.

LET GO OF JUDGMENT

"God did not send his Son into the world to judge the world guilty, but to save the world through him."

JOHN 3:17 NCV

Christ is our greatest example for how we should treat others. He did not come to judge the world or to focus on people's flaws; he came to set the captives free, to heal the sick, and to raise the dead. He came to bring life. He did not nitpick people's flaws. In fact, the only ones he really challenged were those who thought they already knew God but did not live according to his values.

When we let go of judging others and instead look for the ways we appreciate them, our relationships are better for it. Jesus graciously offered restoration and love to those who came to him with earnest hearts. He saw them through the lens of God's love. How would our thoughts toward others and the important relationships in our lives change if we did the same?

When you're tempted to judge someone close to you, choose to see them through the lens of love today. Try to understand where they're coming from. Remember the things you appreciate about them.

SHARE YOUR JOY

Praise the LORD in song, for He has done glorious things;
Let this be known throughout the earth.

ISAIAH 12:5 NASB

Appreciation for God starts in our hearts. When we extend
our gratitude to others, it ripples into the lives of those
people. Our actions and emotions can be contagious;
they can inspire others and catch on in the behavior of
the people around us. This is true of negative emotions
like frustration, but it is also true of positive ones such as
gratitude.

When we are overcome with thankfulness, it transforms
our perspectives. As we share it with others, we pass on the
wonder in our hearts to those who can celebrate with us. It
may even inspire them to look for things they are thankful
for as well. Good news is meant to be shared, so let's be sure
to make ours known to those close to us.

*At this point, you have probably been practicing gratitude
in a myriad of ways. As you reflect on what has impacted
you most, pick one or two practices that you can share with
others and do it today.*

A SLIGHT SHIFT

Put your heart and soul into every activity you do,
as though you are doing it for the Lord himself
and not merely for others.

COLOSSIANS 3:23 TPT

When we are focused on what people aren't doing for us,
all the while feeling like we're giving everything we've got,
it can be discouraging. Differences of opinion can threaten
us when our focus is on being accepted rather than living
authentically. When we redirect our outlook and approach
to living honestly and doing what is truly ours to do
without adding on the extra work of weighing others' input,
we can confidently move ahead.

The Lord is our audience, and if we need the approval of
anyone, we should seek to please him. God sees it all: every
act of surrender, every task accomplished, every offense
laid aside. He sees and he knows. He is pleased with you as
you put your heart and soul into all that you do, and you
don't get sidetracked by the criticisms of others. When you
are more focused on what you are doing rather than the
behaviors of others, you are effectively tending the garden
of your own life.

*God extends mercy and wisdom. When you feel tempted
to rush into the judgment of someone else, refocus your
attention on your own life and all that is yours to do.*

PATIENT ENDURANCE

May the Lord lead your hearts into a full understanding
and expression of the love of God and the patient
endurance that comes from Christ.

2 THESSALONIANS 3:5 NLT

As you incorporate gratitude into your daily habits, you
grow in your understanding of the love that God has for
you in the details of your life. Patient endurance is an effect
of a grounded peace which understands that waiting is not
in vain.

Mental endurance is as important as physical endurance.
Gratitude is shown to build resilience in those who practice
it. That means that we can not only get through the tough
moments of life, but we can also bounce back faster. With
decreased stress and improved cognitive function, the
practice of gratitude makes us capable of withstanding the
hardships of life and moving through them with more peace.

*When you hit a rough patch today in a conversation, a
physical challenge, or a difficult task, practice gratitude to
refocus and get through it.*

EVEN UNDER PRESSURE

We are hard pressed on every side, but not crushed;
perplexed, but not in despair.

2 CORINTHIANS 4:8 NIV

Even under the pressures of life, we can find reasons to
be grateful. A sunny day, a child's laugh, a warm hug—we
have so many good reasons to give thanks. Gratitude can be
incorporated in many ways. Finding what works for you is
helpful when you need it most and you can recall it easily.

Resilience is built through the practice of gratitude because
it helps us know that the stressors of life are not the only
reality. There is also goodness. There is beauty around us
at the same time there is negativity. Good things don't
erase the hardships, but they certainly make them more
bearable. We need the balance of gratitude to ground us
and to remind us that goodness is always present. When we
have that, we can endure the pressures and not succumb to
despair.

*Come up with a short list of things that you are grateful for.
Couple it with a meditative or reflective activity. This can
have a calming effect on the stress responses of our minds
and bodies.*

NOURISHED AND EQUIPPED

"Blessed is the man who trusts in the LORD,
And whose hope is the LORD.
For he shall be like a tree planted by the waters."

JEREMIAH 17:7 NKJV

Nourishment isn't theoretical; it is practical. We don't have to rely on yesterday's bread to get through today. Each day is filled with the fresh mercies of God which meet us where we're at. When we practice gratitude, we look to what is true, good, and beneficial here and now. We don't have to dig into the past or jump into the future.

Trust grows through consistent connection. We don't have to blindly trust God. He is faithful, and he follows through on his promises. If we lean in closely and look for the evidence of his goodness in our lives, we will find it. This is what gratitude helps us do; we learn to tune into the present beauty and to see the things we may take for granted. This makes it easier to release the aspects of our lives that we cannot control.

Take a few moments whether you are in the car, at home, or out for a walk, and notice everything you can see around you that is beneficial to you.

NOTHING OFF LIMITS

This is the confidence we have before him:
If we ask anything according to his will, he hears us.

1 JOHN 5:14 CSB

When we remain focused on certain areas of our lives, we may take other aspects for granted. If we are fixated on growing our career, for instance, we may neglect the relationships in our lives. One area may thrive, but there may be others that suffer. We don't have endless energy, so we need to focus on what is most important in this season.

As we develop our practices of gratitude, we may start to see patterns emerge. What we are most thankful for may change, but we will get a clearer picture of what matters most overall. From this position, we can reassess how we spend our time and what we need to include in our schedules. We have confidence in God when we come to him in prayer, and the truth is that as we lay everything before him, we can pinpoint what feels most poignant to us. Let's take charge of our own schedules and the timing of our day's events, being sure to include the people and things that are important to us.

Evaluate your schedule and be sure to include time for your friends and hobbies.

CLARITY

God is not a God of confusion but of peace.

1 CORINTHIANS 14:33 ESV

When we are overwhelmed, we may find it hard to concentrate. Too much burden can make us worry incessantly and feel as if we are under constant strain. It becomes difficult to enjoy normal activities because we lack focus and are confused about what needs to be done to move ahead. When we are overwhelmed, it is easy to feel a sense of hopelessness. But God offers us relief and clarity in the peacefulness of his presence. His law of love doesn't burden us; it sets us free.

Where we feel constricted, those are the areas where we need the grace of God to meet us. Gratitude can help us escape the fog of confusion by tethering us to the present moment. We are not meant to live with our heads in the clouds, but rather, we need to live with our feet grounded on the earth beneath us. Clarity comes with an expansive sense of peace. There is no need to rush but also no need to procrastinate. Let's spend time grounding our hearts and minds in the peace of God today.

If you begin to feel overwhelmed or with a sense of loss today, take a few minutes to close your eyes and focus on each breath you take. Ask God to fill you with his peace.

SO MUCH GOODNESS

Everything God made is good, and nothing should be
refused if it is accepted with thanks.

1 TIMOTHY 4:4 NCV

The rules and regulations of religious systems can distract
us from the freedom we've been given in Christ. Everything
God made is good. We don't have to worry about dietary
restrictions—except, of course, for allergies—since our
food choices do not reflect our morality for the good or
the bad. Food is nourishment, and as we receive it with
thankfulness, it can be just simply food.

Oftentimes we get distracted by things that don't matter in
the long run, but which keep us from focusing on the areas
that do. If you have a complicated relationship with food,
perhaps one way you can heal that is by taking time before
each meal to thank God for his provision for your body.
Don't get caught up in what others may think or say about
your food choices. Simply receive it with thanks and move
on with your day. If you are hungry, eat. If you are thirsty,
drink. Then you will be able to put your energy toward
things that matter more than what is on your plate.

*Every time you catch yourself questioning whether or not you
should eat something, thank God that you have a choice, and
that nourishment is necessary when you are hungry. Take
each moment before a meal to thank God for his provision.*

FOLLOWING JESUS

"You shall follow the LORD your God and fear Him;
and you shall keep His commandments,
listen to His voice, serve Him, and cling to Him."

DEUTERONOMY 13:4 NASB

Jesus said that the whole of God's law could be summed up simply. "In everything, therefore, treat people the same way you want them to treat you, for this is the Law and the Prophets" (Matthew 7:12). When we treat others the way that we want to be treated, we offer grace, love, patience, and kindness. Think of all the fruits of the Spirit described in Galatians 5. Those are the attributes of one who lives with this in mind.

We can be grateful that the gospel of Christ is simple. It may not be easy to choose love at every turn, but it certainly isn't difficult to understand. Practicing gratitude every day may help us be more kind and patient with others. We are more prone to offering the benefit of the doubt to others rather than rushing into judgment.

When you interact with others today, remember how you would like to be treated if you were in their situation. Choose your attitude accordingly. And when you mess up, admit it!

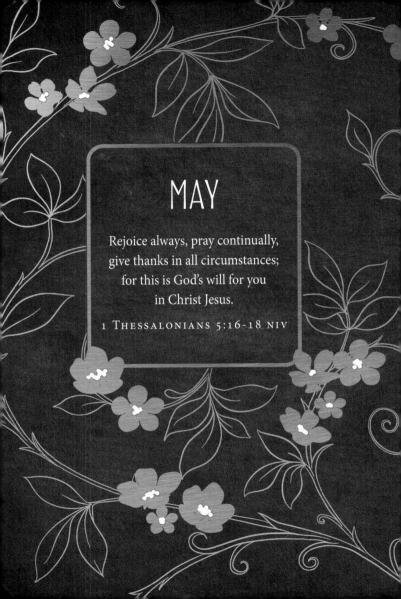

MAY

Rejoice always, pray continually,
give thanks in all circumstances;
for this is God's will for you
in Christ Jesus.

1 Thessalonians 5:16-18 NIV

FIRM FOUNDATION

The Lord Yahweh is always faithful to place you on a firm foundation and guard you from the Evil One.

2 THESSALONIANS 3:3 TPT

No matter where you are, what you're going through, or what you've been through, there is a firm foundation under your feet. Sometimes all you need is a little perspective to see it. That's where the practice of gratitude can be life-altering. It's a reminder of what you should depend upon as the foundation of your life, and it brings a present mindedness to your day which may help you be more engaged.

Gratitude can direct and help us find meaning in the work we do. When we are alert to the good that our accomplishments offer, we will find more satisfaction in what we do. When we realize our agency in how we choose to live and interact with others, there is a sense of empowerment. We can move ahead as we realize that the solid rock of God's grace is underneath us.

Make a list of everything you are grateful for in your work, including the people you serve and the work itself.

TODAY'S THE DAY

"At just the right time, I heard you.
On the day of salvation, I helped you."
Indeed, the "right time" is now.
Today is the day of salvation.

2 CORINTHIANS 6:2 NLT

We cannot live for the future nor stay stuck in the past and
expect to be satisfied with our lives. If we are not connected
to the present moment, we will forever be searching for that
feeling of satisfaction, but it will elude us. Why does the
Word of God say that today is the day of salvation? Because,
in short, it's the only hope we have. Every day is its own gift
and its own opportunity. When we put off the important
things for another time, that time does not come.

Practicing gratitude keeps us connected to the present
moment. It engages us with the opportunities we have now
as we appreciate what has already been so helpful to us.
Gratitude does not have to look complicated or be a drawn-
out process. It can be as simple as observing the goodness
around us whenever we think of it. Today's the day of
salvation, for it is all we have!

*Decide how you will live purposely engaged with today. What
relationships need nurturing? As you move from gratitude
into action, remember that every opportunity is a gift.*

SECURELY HELD

"The eternal God is your refuge,
and underneath are the everlasting arms."

DEUTERONOMY 33:27 NIV

We are made to know others and to be known by them.
We are created for relationships, and those relationships
are gifts of God's goodness. We don't have to be close to
everyone in our lives, and in fact that's not possible, so
investing in our close relationships is a priority.

In times of trouble, we all need safe spaces to rest. God
is our refuge, and he is always available to his people. He
holds us up with the strength of his arms. We can also know
the power of God's presence through the relationships
he has given us in our loyal friends, partners, and family
members. We cannot be everything to one another, but we
can be glimpses of God's love as we support one another in
our times of need.

*Think of someone who has been there for you through a
tough time in your life. Take some time to reach out to them
and thank them for their presence and support.*

GRACIOUS PRESENCE

"In Your great mercy
You did not utterly consume them nor forsake them;
For You are God, gracious and merciful."

NEHEMIAH 9:31 NKJV

God will never forsake or leave us no matter how obstinate we are being or how discouraged we feel. His presence is inescapable, and it is always full of love, joy, peace, patience, and kindness. He is a gentle Savior and a strong and faithful help in times of trouble. As we incorporate gratitude into our daily practices, we build the ability to recognize God's goodness in our lives. He has not left us, and he won't.

Gratitude can give us a sense of relief, knowing that there are more than just hardships present. We cannot escape the tough times of life, but we can know respite amid them. As we practice looking for the goodness that is with us, our eyes naturally look for more. Instead of getting lost in disappointments, we move our attentions to the beauty that remains.

Look for signs of goodness in the world around you. Every flower, every ray of sunshine, every answered prayer—no matter how small it may seem, acknowledge the blessing and treasure it in your heart.

WONDERFULLY MADE

It was you who created my inward parts;
you knit me together in my mother's womb.
I will praise you
because I have been remarkably and wondrously made.
Your works are wondrous,
and I know this very well.

PSALM 139:13-14 CSB

In our practices of gratitude, we can often look outside ourselves. This helps us to root our focus in the world around us, which in turn makes us feel connected to the greater whole. This is a wonderful thing! We should not, however, overlook the goodness, creativity, and unique traits that we ourselves hold. We are each remarkably and wondrously made in the image of God.

The practice of gratitude has been linked to higher self-esteem. We should not resist the confidence of knowing that we are amazing creations made by a good God. In fact, it is in this place of confidence that we can engage with others more wholly. We are not working from a deficit in God's kingdom, but from an abundance. This is true, too, of our own worth!

Stand in front of a mirror and thank God for all that you see. Take some time and thank him for the features you love and the features you struggle with. Don't leave out a thing!

SIMPLE INSTRUCTIONS

"Render true judgments, show kindness and mercy to one another, do not oppress the widow, the fatherless, the sojourner, or the poor, and let none of you devise evil against another in your heart."

ZECHARIAH 7:8-10 ESV

Gratitude helps us see the good in one another, which leads to treating each other more graciously. Mother Theresa famously said, "We cannot do great things on this earth; only small things with great love." Every small kindness is an expression of love lived out.

We should treat those closest to us with kindness, but also those we casually interact with. We can be respectful to co-workers, tip well in restaurants, help someone across the street, volunteer in our communities—the ideas are endless! As we extend mercy to one another, we are as blessed in the giving as those who receive. Let's look for ways to reach out, and then lend a helping hand. In so doing, we live as reflections of Christ's love.

Look for ways to perform a random act of kindness to a stranger.

ASK SEARCH FIND

"Everyone who asks will receive.
The one who searches will find.
And everyone who knocks will have the door opened."

LUKE 11:10 NCV

As we ask, search, and knock, we will find solutions to our questions. Consider what happens when you are thinking about something; you easily spot it even if you aren't looking for it, but far faster if you are. Try it out. Look for yellow things wherever you're at. The more you look, the more you'll find. Have you ever considered buying a new car and suddenly wherever you go, you see the make and model you are looking at? The more attention you pay to something, the more easily you are drawn to it.

Gratitude works in the same way. The more you think about what you're grateful for, the more things will come to mind. It also turns what little you think you have into enough.

Pick something that you want to focus on today and watch how many places it shows up around you.

LIGHT OF LIFE

"I am the Light of the world; the one who follows Me will not walk in the darkness, but will have the Light of life."

JOHN 8:12 NASB

Life is made up of moments. When we feel as if it's hard to gain the life we want, we only need to connect to the places we put our energy in at this moment. This may feel overwhelming if it is too abstract. But consider how we can feel empowered if we choose what is beneficial and have clarity about what is important.

One way to get this clarity is to practice gratitude. When we follow Jesus, it is not without its challenges. However, he does not withhold his nature from us. He is full of loyal love, delight, peace, and hope. As we orient our lives around him, we find the evidence of his Spirit's work around and within us. Gratitude helps us tune in to these workings, and each one is instrumental in anchoring our hearts in hope.

Look for the little rays of delight, presence, and peace that shine into your life today.

UNDERSTOOD

He understands humanity, for as a man, our magnificent
King-Priest was tempted in every way just as we are, and
conquered sin.

HEBREWS 4:15 TPT

It can be hard to share our struggles with people who don't
understand what we're going through. It's not impossible
by any means, but it can feel like a hurdle. We all want to
be seen and known. We don't want to be misunderstood.
Thankfully, Christ understands our humanity because
he himself lived the experience. He understands our
weaknesses. He doesn't hold it against us; rather, he shows
us the way through.

Empathy is a powerful connector. When we imagine
ourselves in the place of another it opens our hearts to
understanding. We build bridges of connection rather than
walls of hostility. Christ came to unify us in his love, and
it is this love that breaks down walls. As we fill our hearts
with gratitude, we create a place for that love to grow.

*When you feel yourself judging someone too quickly, be
proactive, and instead try to understand where they are
coming from.*

RENEWED ATTITUDE

Let the Spirit renew your thoughts and attitudes.

EPHESIANS 4:23 NLT

Gratitude can have a major impact on our mindsets. It can change the way we look at things. This in turn changes our attitudes. Consider what happens when we change our minds about something. As we learn, we adopt different ways of thinking and adapt to the new information. As we integrate these new patterns of thinking into our lives, our perceptions change. This, too, is true of gratitude.

If you spend weeks being thankful for a person with whom you struggle, your attitude toward that person changes over that time. The Spirit renews our thoughts and attitudes as we learn his ways and adopt Christ's wisdom into our experiences. Gratitude is a wonderful way to allow this work to happen. It doesn't ignore reality; it embraces the goodness in it. Gratitude is not wishful thinking; rather, it is connecting to the truth of what is good right here and now, and it helps balance the negative aspects of life.

When you find yourself resenting someone or struggling to be kind to them, pick out one or two things you do appreciate about them and focus on those. It can diffuse your frustration with the negative aspects of your relationship and renew your attitude toward them.

COUNT YOUR JOYS

How can we thank God enough for you in return for all the joy we have in the presence of our God because of you?

1 THESSALONIANS 3:9 NIV

The most fulfilling relationships are the ones that are reciprocal. Though the relationship may vary depending on who pursues whom at times, there is mutual support available. You can depend on them to be there for you when you need it, and vice versa. These are relationships to rejoice over, for they are a blessing from God.

Think of those who have been there throughout your life. Can you rejoice over the relationships that are no longer present and yet still be grateful for what they were at the time? Are you grateful for those relationships you have in your life now? There are many reasons to rejoice in gratitude, and our relationships are a major one!

Think of someone who was there for you in a particularly hard moment in your life. Now consider how you can show them your gratitude. You could send flowers, take them to dinner, or send a card. Whatever it is, be genuine and specific about what you are thankful for and follow through on it!

CHASING AWE

When I consider Your heavens, the work of Your fingers,
The moon and the stars, which You have ordained,
What is man that You are mindful of him,
And the son of man that You visit him?

PSALM 8:3-4 NKJV

There are many ways we can connect to awe. One of the main ways is through creation. Being in nature—driving in the mountains, sitting beside a waterfall, wandering near the ocean, looking up at a starry sky—all this type of activity can calm our nervous systems and connect us to the world. Awe is a powerful emotion. It is both poignant and expansive. Though it is different from gratitude, they are similar, and gratitude can lead us toward it.

Where are the places we feel the most wonder? Is there a particular path, a stream, or spot where we can feel the grandeur of the world and the minuteness of our problems? Prioritizing these experiences, especially when we are overwhelmed, can help us cope with the overwhelming challenges in our lives. Gratitude and awe can go together, especially when we are in a beautiful place that makes us feel the scope of our humanity.

Spend time chasing awe outdoors today. Look at the night sky, go birdwatching in the woods, or sit on your back porch. Engage with nature in a way that helps settle your soul.

RULED BY PEACE

Let the peace of Christ, to which you were also called in one body, rule your hearts. And be thankful.

COLOSSIANS 3:15 CSB

Gratitude can lead us to a more peaceful state of mind. The more we practice it, the more we are reminded that there is goodness present here. When we are constantly striving for something out of our reach, satisfaction and peace may elude us. But when we ground ourselves in the present moment through gratitude, we can experience the power of that moment. We can embrace the beauty of the now.

The presence of Christ is always available, and it is full of the peace of God. God does not worry, and we can trust him with the things that worry us. As we do, and as we notice the gifts which he has already given us, we can rest in his peace. Let's not forget the power of his promises, including the peace that passes all understanding.

Think of everything that helps you rest and brings you peace and thank God for them.

EFFECTS OF ENDURANCE

Let steadfastness have its full effect,
that you may be perfect and complete,
lacking in nothing.

JAMES 1:4 ESV

Steadfastness is defined as possessing the quality of being unwavering. Endurance helps us pass through hard times. Discomfort can make us want a way to escape it, but the truth is that we cannot outrun our experiences. We will have pain and loss in life. These are not the enemy; they are a natural part of it. When we ground ourselves in gratitude, we can endure the hard times with more resolution because we become aware of the reality that the hard things are not all that we have. There is still beauty. There is still value. There are still a lot of reasons to keep going.

Gratitude connects us to those things. It redirects our attention to what remains good, true, and lovely, even amid the hardships. In the end, we become satisfied, not when everything is right in our world, but when we embrace all that is already here and available to us.

When you feel uncomfortable today, instead of trying to escape the sensation, push through it while allowing the feelings that come up. Remember that you are strong in the Lord, and you can do difficult things.

LIVING SACRIFICE

Since God has shown us great mercy, I beg you to offer your lives as a living sacrifice to him. Your offering must be only for God and pleasing to him, which is the spiritual way for you to worship.

ROMANS 12:1 NCV

Becoming a living sacrifice to the Lord does not mean never experiencing joy, pleasure, or satisfaction. In fact, joy is accessible right now through the practice of gratitude. Life satisfaction is shown to increase with the developed habit of thankfulness. What a beautiful truth this is. There are treasures of delight to be found in the nitty-gritty of our lives. We access them through our attention and our gratitude.

Studies have shown that depressive symptoms may reduce when we create daily practices of gratitude. This is not to say that we should avoid other interventions, but by incorporating gratitude into our lives, we can vastly improve our outlooks and the quality of our lives.

Put a reminder to direct your attention to gratitude in a prominent place in your home. Make it visible on a mirror, inside your front door, or at eye-level on your fridge.

PERFECT GIFTS

Every good thing given and every perfect gift is from above, coming down from the Father of lights, with whom there is no variation or shifting shadow.

JAMES 1:17 NASB

Every good thing is from above. This means that every good thing in our lives is worth celebrating because it is a blessing from God. Nothing is too small to not be a reason for rejoicing. No gift should be overlooked. Gratitude helps us connect with both the big and the small gifts that are all around us.

When we focus our attention on the goodness that is already present in our lives, we honor the giver of those gifts. Delight in the little joys today, and you may just find that your heart is more full, more peaceful, and more satisfied. God gives generously and without hidden motives. There are no shifting shadows in his heart or his presence. As you acknowledge the beautiful parts of your life, allow your heart to overflow in gratitude to the Lord.

Find a way to give a gift just for the joy of it today. Bless someone with a meal, coffee, or a meaningful note. Be creative and intentional and do it without expecting anything in return.

BEAUTY OF BELONGING

We, your devoted lovers, will forever thank you,
praising your name from generation to generation!

PSALM 79:13 TPT

Gratitude doesn't only connect us to the Lord; it also connects us to others. He is a good Father, and he has welcomed us into his family. We are not isolated or alone even if we may feel that way from time to time. Gratitude helps us see the connections that are already there instead of focusing on what we don't have.

A few genuine friends are better than many superficial ones. Having people in your life that you can rely on is a gift from God. We can find the depth of our chosen family within our friendships as well as in our communities. Being seen, accepted, and challenged by those who know us well is one of the greatest aspects of life. Let's not neglect the life-giving relationships we have. Let's look at them with gratitude and thank the faithful people in our lives.

Think of those you are closest to and the specific ways you are grateful for those relationships. Make a point of expressing your gratitude for their presence in your life in some way today.

CHOSEN OFFERINGS

I will sacrifice a voluntary offering to you;
I will praise your name, O Lord,
for it is good.

PSALM 54:6 NLT

Our expressions of gratitude along with the things we are thankful for, are as unique to us as our own personalities. None of us is the same, and we should not treat the practice of gratitude as a replicable blueprint. Use whatever method of expression that works for you and whatever connects with your heart and mind and change it up if you need to. Gratitude is simply the quality of being thankful. That means this quality can be engaged with and expressed in a multitude of ways.

Perhaps you are tired of making gratitude lists and instead want to artfully express your thankfulness. You could make a collage, start a photo series, or paint with your favorite colors. You could write a melody, dance to a favorite song, or simply engage in an activity you enjoy. Let your heart lead you to whatever expression brings you connection to God and joy in your life!

Choose a creative new way to express your gratitude through an activity of your choosing.

IN EVERY SITUATION

Do not be anxious about anything, but in every situation,
by prayer and petition, with thanksgiving, present your
requests to God.

PHILIPPIANS 4:6 NIV

Prayer is a powerful way to connect to both the present
moment and to the presence of God. When anxiety is
heightened, the practice of gratitude helps us let go of the
worries and to trust God with what we cannot control.
When we turn our attention to the things that have not
changed—the steadfast relationships, the faithfulness of
God throughout our histories, the inevitable passing of
momentary troubles—we can find rest and peace.

Whatever troubles come up, bring them to God in prayer.
Do you have worries about any uncertainties you face?
Pray. Do you have a problem that you don't know how to
solve? Pray. Do you have joy overflowing? Praise God and
pray. Every reason, every situation, every kind of emotion,
absolutely everything, is an avenue to connect with God
through prayer.

*Prayer is a powerful tool of gratitude. It directs our
attentions outside ourselves while also giving us space to
express what is within us. Take time to pray as often as you
think of it. God cares about it all!*

MOVED BY MUSIC

Sing to the LORD with thanksgiving;
Sing praises on the harp to our God.

PSALM 147:7 NKJV

Music is a wonderful gift that is beyond the boundaries of words. It connects to our souls as well as our bodies. It can move us to dance or to tears. It can fill us with hope, awe, or grief. There is a reason that movies and television shows implement music: it adds to a scene's emotions. It can even direct us to perceive the actors' interactions in orchestrated ways determined by the writers and producers.

Many of us still remember the words to songs we learned as children. Music helps us connect to ourselves in ways that otherwise would be forgotten. Consider the effect music has on people with dementia. Although these patients may not remember the faces of their loved ones, in many instances they can sing along to the songs of their youth.

Give your gratitude a playlist today by listening to songs that remind you of wonderful times, people you love, or even simply the awesomeness of God.

RADIANT EXPRESSIONS

The Son is the radiance of God's glory and the exact
expression of his nature, sustaining all things by his
powerful word. After making purification for sins, he sat
down at the right hand of the Majesty on high.

HEBREWS 1:3 CSB

One of the best ways we can connect to the power of Christ
is through gratitude for who he is: friend, teacher, Lord,
guide, and the sacrifice for our sins. Knowing that Christ
is the exact expression of God's nature, we can confidently
thank him for the mercy he shows and the freedom he offers.

As we experience the wonders of God's love for us, we are
recipients of his goodness at work in the world. We need
to look no further than the ministry of Jesus to find what
God is truly like. He is not power-hungry, elitist, or cruel.
He is humble, gentle, and overflowing in compassion. What
radiant expressions of goodness we find in Christ!

*Read through part of the gospels today for a refresher
on what Jesus is like. When you find an attribute of his
character that you are grateful for, write it down.*

CLOTHED IN COMPASSION

Put on then, as God's chosen ones,
holy and beloved, compassionate hearts,
kindness, humility, meekness, and patience.

COLOSSIANS 3:12 ESV

Interestingly, both gratitude and compassion are connected to how we interact with others. Gratitude may be cultivated privately, but it affects how we engage with others in our lives. Compassion is a connective force that moves us to help relieve the suffering of others. When we clothe our hearts in compassion, therefore, we are choosing kindness and helpfulness in order to bless those around us.

Gratitude doesn't have to remain a private practice. Although only we can take ownership of our own perspectives, we can also make active engagement with people easier through practical acts of gratitude. God's love should not remain just a nice ideal. It is shown through purposeful living with choices that demonstrate active love. The same is true of gratitude. The more we engage with the things that we are thankful for in life, the more motivated we will be to show that to others.

Relate to others within the truth of their sometimes-difficult circumstances. Look for even one small way to offer them relief.

DANCING IN CELEBRATION

David danced with all his might before the LORD. He had on a holy linen vest. David and all the Israelites shouted with joy and blew the trumpets as they brought the Ark of the LORD to the city.

2 SAMUEL 6:14-15 NCV

Many cultures celebrate with dance. This is true in public ceremonies, but it also shows up in private homes. Dancing can be a wonderful way to rejoice with others. King David danced before the Lord in his personal worship, and we can do the same. We can also dance with our friends and in our communities.

Whether at a wedding, a school dance, or an informal get-together, dance is an opportunity to connectively engage with our joy in the expressions of our bodies. It shouldn't be reserved for professionals. It is our right to move our bodies to the rhythms of music as an expression of our emotions. Consider how you can reflect your gratitude through movement today, for it can be a powerful tool to embody your thankfulness.

Put on a favorite song and dance simply for the joy of it!

EYES OPENED

I pray that the eyes of your heart may be enlightened, so that you will know what is the hope of His calling, what are the riches of the glory of His inheritance in the saints.

EPHESIANS 1:18 NASB

Often our eyes are opened to other points of view not by accident, but rather through a willingness to learn. We are exposed to various opinions and mindsets through interactions with those who are different than us. Fellowship with the Holy Spirit leaves an open line to his wisdom. When we humble our hearts before him, we allow ourselves to admit that we do not know everything. This can lead to a change in perspective as God reveals his wisdom to us.

We can prime our hearts for this kind of perspective shift by regularly practicing a viewpoint that sees people and circumstances differently. Gratitude takes our focus off the negative aspects of life and opens our awareness to the beauty that is around us. The more we practice it, the more we see. The more we see, the more our perspectives are transformed. Our expectations grow in experiencing the goodness of God meeting us where we are at. What a wonderful way to live!

Look for the little surprises of beauty and goodness around you. Every time you find one, thank God for it.

LIGHT OF HIS PRESENCE

If we keep living in the pure light that surrounds him, we share unbroken fellowship with one another, and the blood of Jesus, his Son, continually cleanses us from all sin.

1 JOHN 1:7 TPT

When you think of light, what comes to mind? Do you think of a sunrise or the bright noonday sun? Take some time to meditate on what light is. Think about what it feels like, what it does, and how it affects your thoughts.

Darkness may evoke fear in some people, but the light diminishes the fear. Though much of the future remains in the dark, the light of God's presence is with us now. It goes with us each moment into that dark future, and it will not stop. Every step will be lit up with his peace and the light of his countenance. We don't have to fear anything because he is already living all of time in full awareness it. Instead of fearing whatever is to come, we can connect to the light of God's presence as it meets us now. Everything we need is already in this moment. Let's not get ahead of ourselves, but instead let's dwell in the peace of his presence in this very moment.

Whenever you start to feel overwhelmed by thoughts of the future, bring your awareness to what is true, lovely, and sufficient in the present moment.

INCREASING LOVE

May the Lord make your love for one another
and for all people grow and overflow.

1 THESSALONIANS 3:12 NLT

One sure way to increase our love for one another is to see the goodness in each other. When we call out the things we love about others, we are drawn to see them in that positive light. Perfection is unattainable, but loving people as they are is certainly an attainable goal. We can love others well when we accept them and are grateful for who they are.

Much like a bad mood can be passed on to others, so can gratitude. When we take the time to express the blessing that someone is to us, both parties' benefit. Instead of focusing on the frustrations we have with others; we can redirect our thoughts in gratitude. When we do, we build a case for their goodness in our own hearts. This can help our relationships tremendously, and focusing on the negatives will most assuredly will do them harm.

Focus on the things you love and appreciate about the people around you, especially when you find yourself becoming frustrated with them.

CONFIDENCE IN CHRIST

In him and through faith in him we may approach God
with freedom and confidence.

EPHESIANS 3:12 NIV

Freedom is a wonderful thing. And though we may feel
freedom in some aspects of our lives, the truth is that most
of us feel constricted and controlled in other areas. A lack
of freedom makes us feel stuck. There are, however, ways in
which we may be able to change the narrative.

To be sure, we cannot transmute a prison sentence by
wishful thinking. But we can look at what our options are
and choose something workable within that scope. We can
be incredibly free on the inside if we recognize the areas
where we still have agency over our lives, perspectives, and
choices. Even in a prison cell, there are choices to be made.
Thankfully, one thing we need never question is whether we
can come to God as we are. We can come confidently and
freely before him anywhere and at any time. He receives us
with grace and mercy each time we do.

*When you feel as if you're without options, look a little
deeper. Perhaps you feel stuck because you are trying to fit
into someone else's expectations. You have the freedom to
choose how you will live today. Start with gratitude and live
it out.*

LOVE-MINDED

If there is any consolation in Christ, if any comfort of love,
if any fellowship of the Spirit, if any affection and mercy,
fulfill my joy by being like-minded, having the same love,
being of one accord, of one mind.

PHILIPPIANS 2:1-2 NKJV

The Bible does not tell us to be like-minded in our political
views or with our opinions on popular culture. It does,
however, advise us to be like-minded in terms of having
the same love. This is an important distinction, especially
in an age where everything seems to delineate the lines
of division ever clearer. We can disagree about things and
still love one another well. Christ does not ask us to be the
same; he asks us to be united in love.

We should not use our platforms to promote hate. We
should be quick to give others the benefit of the doubt,
forgive those who offend us, and extend kindness to those
with whom we disagree. Let's be wary of any pressure to fall
in line on various opinions. Consider how Paul addressed
the freedom of food to a group who was biased toward
religious restrictions. Let's be quick to approach others with
love, just as Christ did.

*When you feel yourself judging others, remember that you
have a choice in how you view them. Treat them the way you
would like to be treated.*

REWRITE YOUR HEART

Never let loyalty and faithfulness leave you.
Tie them around your neck;
write them on the tablet of your heart.

PROVERBS 3:3 CSB

The imagery in this proverb is a powerful one. We can write things on the tablet of our hearts; we get to choose what we focus on. When we prioritize the loyalty and faithfulness of God, we engrave our hearts with these elements. As we choose to focus on gratitude, we do the same.

One of the ways we do this is by curating what we pay attention to. This is easier said than done in the real world but consider the ways you can do this in your electronic feeds. Social media can be a tool that drains us, but it can also be used to promote positivity. We get to choose who we follow, whose influence we want to pay attention to, and how long we spend with these media. Being mindful about our feeds is one easy way to include more gratitude in how we engage with technology.

If you are on social media, unfollow accounts that don't add to your peace or gratitude. Be sure to follow ones that help you to recognize goodness in the world. Also remember to be gracious and grateful in your posts.

GENTLE TEACHER

"Take my yoke upon you, and learn from me,
for I am gentle and lowly in heart,
and you will find rest for your souls."

MATTHEW 11:29 ESV

Jesus' invitation for us to find rest in him is as applicable today as it was when he first uttered these words. The Spirit of God offers us peace as we offer him the weighty things in our lives, our minds, and our hearts. We can trust Jesus. He is gentle and humble, and he is patient with us. His love is abundant. There is always more than enough in the generous love of his heart for us.

Think of the people in your life who have impacted you the most. Have they been harsh taskmasters, or have they been gracious? Chances are you have more than one person in mind and their temperaments are varied. Even so, Jesus is a gentle teacher, and he motivates us with love. He offers us what we need, and he does not withhold it until we prove ourselves. There is no better expression of gratitude than offering the same love to others!

Thank God for the gentle, patient, and loving teachers in your life. Show your gratitude by offering grace and patience to others today.

LIGHTER

"The burden that I ask you to accept is easy;
the load I give you to carry is light."

MATTHEW 11:30 NCV

As we offer God the heavy load of our worries and cares,
he shares his light load with us. No matter what we are
carrying, what he offers us is lighter. It is full of peace, joy,
and love. All the fruits of the Spirit are found in him. As
we fellowship with him, we become more like him in our
efforts to emulate his goodness in our own lives.

Consider a time when you were surprised by goodness.
Maybe you had relief in not having to deal with an
issue that you thought you would have to, or you got
an unexpected gift that blessed you. Gratitude for your
unexpected blessings can remind you that gifts of grace
appear as God gives them in his own perfect timing. If you
are carrying the weight of worry, lay it down and leave it
with Christ by focusing on whatever you have to be grateful
for today.

*As you let go of your worries, focus on whatever goodness
there is before you. Plan how you can surprise someone else
with an unexpected gift.*

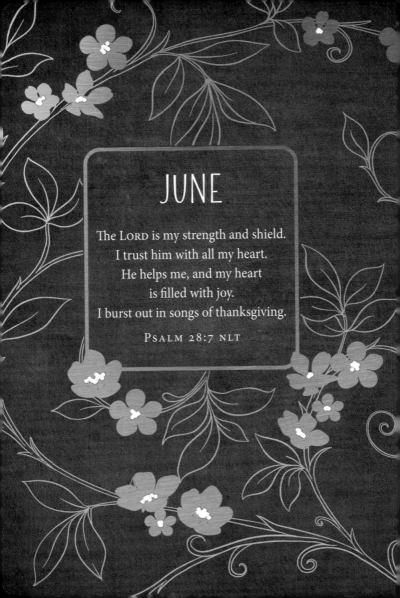

JUNE

The LORD is my strength and shield.
I trust him with all my heart.
He helps me, and my heart
is filled with joy.
I burst out in songs of thanksgiving.

PSALM 28:7 NLT

GRATITUDE THROUGH HOSPITALITY

Do not neglect hospitality to strangers, for by this some have entertained angels without knowing it.

HEBREWS 13:2 NASB

Hospitality is a practical way we can show gratitude for what we have by sharing it with others. We don't have to have a picture-perfect home in order to open it up to others. In the space of our homes, we can experience the strengthening of friendships while serving others.

Hospitality can be simple. We don't even have to cook a meal. We can invite people over for tea or coffee, a conversation, or a game. We can have a small gathering where we exchange plant cuttings, have a clothing swap, or discuss ways to improve the neighborhood. It doesn't have to solely happen within our homes. We can offer hospitality by bringing someone else a meal or by offering a housewarming gift. We can provide food or necessities for someone experiencing homelessness. Truly, hospitality is an expression of generosity and gratitude that matters more than what exactly is given.

Choose one act of hospitality to follow through on this week.

POWERFUL REVELATIONS

What does the lavish supply of the Holy Spirit in your life and the miracles of God's tremendous power have to do with you keeping religious laws? The Holy Spirit is poured out upon us through the revelation and power of faith!

GALATIANS 3:5 TPT

The Holy Spirit's work in our lives is not dependent upon us keeping to the letter of the Law. No, the Spirit moves through us with revelation and in faith. When we don't know what to do, there is wisdom and revelation for us in his fellowship. When we are at a loss, the Spirit's abundance is always overflowing.

Gratitude is a practice that doesn't require us to do more. We just need to tune in more to what is already true. The same can be said of our spiritual lives. We don't have to earn our place in God's kingdom. We already have it. We have only to tune in to the presence of Christ that is already with us to experience the life-giving light of his love and to reap all the benefits just waiting for us.

Every time you give thanks for something today, also thank God that he is in that blessing.

WHAT HE WANTED

God decided in advance to adopt us into his own family by bringing us to himself through Jesus Christ. This is what he wanted to do, and it gave him great pleasure.

EPHESIANS 1:5 NLT

When we are aware of the good things that others think about us, it is so encouraging to our souls. When we are loved and accepted, our self-worth can feel stronger than in the times we are unsure about those things. When others express gratitude for us, we feel seen and acknowledged. What we do and who we are matters, and we know it.

It is important to make sure the people in our lives know how much they mean to us. God sent Christ so that we would know the length and breadth of his love for us. How can we show those in our lives that we choose them, honor them, and love them? Perhaps an act of gratitude is all it takes to strengthen our bonds today.

Whether it is a friend, a family member, or someone you work with, let them know how much you appreciate who they are to you and that the role they have in your life matters.

SOMETHING NEW

I will sing a new song to you, my God;
on the ten-stringed lyre I will make music to you.

PSALM 144:9 NIV

Every day is an opportunity to find fresh ways to engage
with the world and with the people in our lives. If the
same ways of relating feel stale, we have only to look for
inspiration in the originality of nature. The sun sets every
day, but no two sunsets are the same. Snowflakes, flowers,
rivers, and mountains are similar but unique. We may
try to say things a little differently, use songs as a form of
connection, or simply go out of our way to be kind.

New doesn't have to mean completely original. New can
mean just doing things in a way we haven't done them
before. If you are a musician, you probably don't want to
play the same songs repeatedly without periodically adding
new songs. Learning one new thing or changing a routine
in a small way can make all the difference between same-
old and a fresh approach.

*What is a new thing you've been meaning to implement into
your life, or you've wanted to learn? Take some time today
to put action behind the intention. Try something new and
thank God that you can still learn new things.*

SO MANY BLESSINGS

Blessed be the God and Father of our Lord Jesus Christ, who has blessed us with every spiritual blessing in the heavenly places in Christ.

EPHESIANS 1:3 NKJV

There are blessings all around us. If we open our eyes to the goodness that is available to us, we will have a bounty of gratitude to offer back to God. He offers us spiritual blessings, but he also blesses us in very practical ways. If we have food in our bellies, homes to shelter in, and loved ones we call dear, what treasures we already have!

When we learn to embrace the littlest blessings, everything becomes an opportunity to praise God. Ponder one of your happiest memories. Remember the way your heart felt and the energy that surged through your body at the time. Soak in it and engage with that feeling all over again. What a blessing it is to know that the goodness we've experienced is not reserved for only a moment. For as long as we have our memories we can engage with the blessing. Gratitude can span a lifetime as we connect to the goodness of God in our daily lives. The more we look, the more we'll find!

Meditate on a moment when you felt immense gratitude. As you connect to that feeling, allow yourself to be embodied by it once more.

WELLSPRING OF LIFE

The wellspring of life is with you.
By means of your light we see light.

PSALM 36:9 CSB

God is the fountain of life and the wellspring from which we all draw. Christ said that if we will come to him and drink the water he offers, we will experience everlasting life. His living water satisfies our souls eternally.

There is no shame in needing a refreshing encounter with the presence of God. He offers us peace, restoration, and joy as we come to him time and time again. Every day is a fresh opportunity to drink from his well. Instead of living off yesterday's portion, there is a new one awaiting us today. We only have to take, eat, and drink. His grace is generous, and it meets us in fresh waves each new day. Gratitude can help us connect to this by engaging with the moment as it is. As we slow down and connect to our lives and the goodness within, we can feast on God with us: his life with us and his light in our lives.

Spend time in God's presence through prayer, silence, or meditation on the Scriptures. Ask him to fill you with all you need today.

PRIVATE PRACTICE

"When you pray, go into your room and shut the door and pray to your Father who is in secret. And your Father who sees in secret will reward you."

MATTHEW 6:6 ESV

Spirituality starts as a private practice. What we do in private pours into our interactions with others. If we are more concerned about how we are perceived by others than we are by the work of our own spiritual growth, we become distracted away from our most important priorities.

What we do in private becomes the building blocks of our lives. What we pray in secret is seen by God. The hard work we put in behind the scenes is what prepares us to move ahead publicly. Let's not overlook the power of private practice, for it can fuel the more visible areas of our lives. We are seen and known in secret as well as in the open by the God who created us. He recognizes what others overlook. He will not forget a movement of mercy, an act of surrender, or the work that you so diligently put in when no one else is watching.

Let the gratitude from your heart flow to God today. Even if no one else hears the words you speak to him, he does. He honors them.

PLEASING THOUGHTS

I hope my words and thoughts please you.
LORD, you are my Rock, the one who saves me.

PSALM 19:14 NCV

Gratitude helps direct our thoughts to what is pleasant and beneficial. As we look for the beauty in our lives and in the people around us, our attention is turned toward goodness.

If you want to think better thoughts, you must be aware of your influences. What are you reading, listening to, and mentally consuming? These will affect you for better or for worse. If you find yourself gripped with fear and anger, perhaps it's time to evaluate where that may be stemming from. As a simple directive, the practice of gratitude can help to change the way you think by priming your thoughts to seek the positives. This is such a powerful tool that costs us nothing but our time and attention.

Think about the things that inspire you with awe, gratitude, and mindfulness. Incorporate thoughts of these into your daily ritual over the next week and see how that helps your gratitude practice. If you need some ideas, consider reading poetry, looking at art, walking in nature, and spending time with a child.

HELPFUL REFLECTIONS

I remember the days of old;
I meditate on all Your accomplishments;
I reflect on the work of Your hands.

PSALM 143:5 NASB

One of the key elements in leading a more thankful life is to embrace your setbacks. It's a good thing to remember your hard times and how you weathered those storms. The fact that you suffered and yet lived through it is proof of your resilience. It helps your overall gratefulness by giving you a healthy perspective when you are struggling to still find things to be positive about.

Though it may seem counterintuitive, reflecting on harder times can help you feel more grateful for your life as it is now. Perhaps you are living a dream you once had; maybe you wanted a good job or a beautiful home and now you have it. Though life is not perfect, it's as full as you had hoped it would be. When we take the need for perfection out of our expectations, we can embrace our lives for what they are. The gifts we now have are not second-rate even if they look different from what we imagined.

Spend some time reflecting on a hard time in your life. What didn't you have then that you had wished for, and now you do? As you weigh the positives that are yours, you can be thankful for the changes in your life.

HEALTH TO THE BODY

As you unwrap my words,
they will impart true life and radiant health
into the very core of your being.

PROVERBS 4:22 TPT

Studies have shown that those who practice gratitude
have fewer aches and pains as well as lower blood pressure
over time. In short, being intentional about incorporating
gratitude into our lives can help our bodies be healthier.

God's wisdom was always meant for our good. It brings
true life and radiant health to our beings from the inside
out. This doesn't mean we won't ever experience health
issues. It is true, though, that their effects may be less
noticeable as we train our minds to look for the goodness
around us. If all we ever do is focus on the negatives, those
health concerns will grow in our minds. Stress may cause
blood pressure to rise, but if we balance the hard parts of
life with gratitude for the good, we may know the benefits
of boosted health including better pain tolerance!

*Even if you have physical limitations, you can focus on what
you are able to do. Take time today while doing the ordinary
things in your day to give thanks for the ability to do them.
As an example, I am thankful for the ability to use my fingers
to type this sentence.*

PSYCHOLOGY AND PHYSICALITY

"Physical training is good, but training for godliness is much better, promising benefits in this life and in the life to come."

1 TIMOTHY 4:8 NLT

Some studies have shown that physical fitness and gratitude are linked. One study showed that people who practice gratitude will also spend time working out more often than those who don't. They are also less likely to suffer from dietary restrictions and substance abuse issues. Though the causation isn't clear, the correlation still seems to be. Our mental habits can affect our physical ones.

Moving our bodies can even become a part of our gratitude practices. As we are thankful for the strength and resilience in our bodies, we may take better care of them. Moving our bodies is good for our mental health as well as our physical health. If we are feeling angsty, a good workout can help us move through that feeling and get to one of empowerment. Let's not neglect the connection between our brains and our bodies today.

Go for a brisk walk or find a way to move your body that helps you go from overthinking your concerns to simplifying your thoughts. Any high intensity movement should do it.

LEVELS OF TRUST

"Whoever can be trusted with very little can also be trusted
with much, and whoever is dishonest with very little will
also be dishonest with much."

LUKE 16:10 NIV

Trust is something that is built over time and through
shared experiences. We trust strangers less than we do
well-known friends. That's because we don't have enough
information about their characters. Context builds
connection, and time and circumstances are needed for that
to grow. We should be wise about who we share the most
sacred parts of ourselves with. It is wise to let that trust
build naturally.

Jesus said that those who can be trusted with a little can also
be trusted with much. Our characters are tested through
many different areas in life. How we treat others, what we
do with our resources, and the values we build reveal truths
about ourselves. As we engage with gratitude, we can clearly
see the generosity of what we already have and the areas we
may need to work on strengthening over time.

Who in your life has proven themselves trustworthy?
What are the things about them that you're grateful for?
Tell them today.

WORKING TOGETHER

We know that all things work together for good to those
who love God, to those who are the called according
to His purpose.

ROMANS 8:28 NKJV

Gratitude gives us the perspective to see how things work
together for our good. Perhaps our plans fall apart, but we
know that God's goodness never does. We are not suddenly
without his mercy or help. His presence is as powerful
today as it is when we feel closest to him.

Practicing thankfulness every day in specific, practical ways
is what gives us the eyes to see the thread of God's mercy
running through our lives. What we give our attention
to is how we see the world. If we give our attention to the
search for reasons to be thankful, we find them. A practice
of gratitude develops when we learn to manage the areas
we invest in with our attention. As we take time to draw
our focus to the present reality, we ground ourselves in the
moment. As we ground ourselves in the moment, we can
focus on what is true right now. We see what is enough and
what is life giving.

*Take three deep breaths. Close your eyes and focus on the
room you are in, the ground beneath you, and the supports
around you. With each breath, give thanks for having all you
need in this moment.*

HOLY PATIENCE

The Lord does not delay his promise, as some understand delay, but is patient with you, not wanting any to perish but all to come to repentance.

2 PETER 3:9 CSB

When waiting periods feel as if they'll never end, our patience can grow thin. When we keep our perspectives narrow, we may feel confused or frustrated by the lack of forward movement. Though we may not understand why we must wait, gratitude helps us find beauty in the moment and the discomfort of delayed gratification gets easier to deal with.

Children are notorious for wanting things right away. They don't understand the wisdom of waiting, though most parents have reasons for imposing a delay. When we trust that God is a good Father and he knows what he is doing, we can more easily be patient with waiting. We don't have to sit around and twiddle our thumbs. If we only focus on the fact that we must wait, the agitation of our impatience will grow. However, if we accept that there is a purpose in the practice of patience, we can engage with other joys already available to us.

Is there something you are waiting and hoping for? Acknowledging the wait does not mean defeat. Offer it to the Lord in prayer and then spend time recognizing a few things you enjoy about your life as it is today.

AWAKENED TO GOODNESS

Open my eyes, that I may behold
wondrous things out of your law.

PSALM 119:18 ESV

There is only this moment. There is only today. Until, of course, tomorrow comes. But then it is today all over again. We should not neglect learning from the past or building toward the future, but we also must engage in the power of the present. It is the only thing we can do anything about.

When we begin to open our eyes to the beauty of the world around us even with its complexities, gratitude grows in our hearts with that increasing awareness. We must pay attention and look for reasons to be grateful, though the more we do it the more natural it becomes. Let's not neglect the power of the present moment and its opportunity to engage with the wonders and beauty of God and his created world.

Write a poem about something you are grateful for today. Consider sharing it with someone.

GOOD PLANS

"I say this because I know what I am planning for you," says
the LORD. "I have good plans for you, not plans to hurt you.
I will give you hope and a good future."

JEREMIAH 29:11 NCV

If we believe that the best days of our lives are behind us,
we can experience a sense of hopelessness about the future.
The best place to connect to gratitude is in the present
moment, but that does not mean that it doesn't affect our
perspectives about our past and our future. Connecting to
the goodness that is in our lives presently helps us feel more
peaceful today and more optimistic for the future.

We cannot account for the unexpected, but we can trust
that the Lord is with us in every moment. He offers us
strength in our weaknesses, hope in our disappointments,
and joy in the mundane. When we feel overwhelmed by
life, shifting our perspectives to a foundation in gratitude
can help connect us to the presence of God. He will never
leave us or forsake us.

*Today, like every other day, will pass. Hard days and good
days both have their time, but gratitude can make even
the worst days tolerable. Focusing on the blessings can shift
your outlook to the good that is in your life now. Pick one
gratitude point to anchor your thoughts throughout the day.*

HINTS OF HOPE

Faith is the certainty of things hoped for,
a proof of things not seen.

HEBREWS 11:1 NASB

Research suggests that when we give back to others through service or acts of kindness, we become more grateful. Volunteering can give us a sense of purpose, and its motivation being outward focused helps us detach from our introspective narratives. If we want to reconnect with hope, one way to practically move toward that is to help others.

It can be easy to be discouraged by the state of humanity when we observe it from a distance, but when we are engaged in helping others, we see glimpses of goodness in those around us. There are good things happening in the world and good people giving of themselves to help others. We can be a part of the solution by engaging in our communities in practical ways.

Look for a way to serve others whether that is through a volunteer position in a local organization, helping a neighbor in need, or finding service opportunities in your community.

FAITHFUL WITH THE LITTLE THINGS

"Commending his servant, the master replied, 'You have done well, and proven yourself to be my loyal and trustworthy servant. Because you have been a faithful steward to manage a small sum, now I will put you in charge of much, much more. You will experience the delight of your master, who will say to you, "Enter into the joy of your Lord!"

MATTHEW 25:21 TPT

Building toward a dream requires many small steps. Little by little, structures are built. They don't go up overnight, at least not ones that will last. It can be overwhelming to look at all it will take to get from point A to point B. However, when we break it down into manageable steps and focus on the next item on the list, it becomes much more doable.

Gratitude gives us eyes to see the value of the little things. As we engage with the small parts of our lives, a bigger reach is built over time. Instead of getting lost in the theory of what we want with our lives, we must be practical and do the work that is ours to do now if we want to move ahead in any area.

What little but important things have you been overlooking by putting your time toward other items that need your attention? Make those little things a priority today.

LARGE RETURNS

"Though you started with little,
you will end with much."

JOB 8:7 NLT

Faithfulness in day-to-day details adds up to a rich life. Integrity is better than fortune, for good character is more valuable than possessions. When we become people who stand by our word, when we serve others in love, and we use our gifts to benefit others and not only ourselves, but we are also aligning our values with those of God's kingdom.

Small intentions lead us to breakthroughs if we follow through with them. When we align our habits with our values, we put them to work in our lives. Gratitude helps us see things that we might otherwise miss. Small beginnings are nothing to be scoffed at; they should be embraced. Everyone starts somewhere, and today we can only work with what we have. What a gift this is!

As you do the small tasks, thank God for the ability to do them and for the power of persistence to keep doing them.

FOCUSED ON TODAY

"Do not worry about tomorrow,
for tomorrow will worry about itself.
Each day has enough trouble of its own."

MATTHEW 6:34 NIV

Each day not only has enough trouble, as Jesus put it, but also enough goodness of its own. There are opportunities to embrace life just the way it is today. When we jump ahead of ourselves, especially with worries, we distract ourselves from the beauty that is available right here.

The practice of gratitude helps us engage with the present moment. It helps us redirect our focus from our concerns about the future to the grace we have here and now. It is not easy to remain engaged in the present when we're not used to it, but the practice of gratitude helps bring our attention back to today. As we ground ourselves in gratitude, we can more easily let go of the things we cannot control.

When you feel yourself getting ahead today, get up and walk into another room. Pay attention to what is around you. Whisper your gratitude to God for each good thing you find.

PRESENT COMFORT

Though I walk through the valley of the shadow of death,
I will fear no evil;
For You are with me;
Your rod and Your staff, they comfort me.

PSALM 23:4 NKJV

Through companionship we learn the power of support
in hard times as well as the good ones. Though grief, pain,
and suffering can feel lonely at times, we are not actually
meant to bear it alone. The Oxford dictionary's definition of
comfort is, "the alleviation or easing of a person's feelings of
grief or distress." Relief comes in many forms, but it is often
found in a place of being seen, known, and cared for.

Hard times can feel isolating. It is important that in our
gratitude practices, we don't stay insular. When we put
our gratitude into action, we can offer comfort to others.
Think of a time when someone's presence or thoughtfulness
changed your day or came at just the right moment. The
power of intention and the expression of love and care can
do more than we fully understand.

*Reach out to someone you know is having a tough time. Send
a note, a gift, or just offer your presence and a listening ear.
Remember what it was like to receive such care and, with
gratitude, offer it to another.*

PROMISED HELP

"Do not fear, for I am with you;
do not be afraid, for I am your God.
I will strengthen you; I will help you;
I will hold on to you with my righteous right hand."

ISAIAH 41:10 CSB

A person's word is only as good as their follow-through. Consistency in relationships matters greatly. God is faithful, and his help is always there when we need it. He does not shift or change. He does not manipulate or overpromise. He is always good, always near, and always true to his Word.

Focus your gratitude today on a time when you received the help you needed. What circumstances were you experiencing? What troubles were you facing? In the moment you received help, what did that mean to you and how did you respond? Offer your gratitude to those involved and to God for his mercy through it all.

When you see opportunities to help someone in a way that you are able, act on it. This can be your expression of gratitude for what you have, for times when you received help, and for the Lord's presence with you to see a need and be able to meet it.

THE POWER OF STILLNESS

"Be still, and know that I am God.
I will be exalted among the nations,
I will be exalted in the earth!"

PSALM 46:10 ESV

Incorporating times of stillness into our personal practices is so good for our souls, minds, and bodies. Whether we use meditation, walks in nature, or breathing work to disengage from the noise of the world, the power of stillness can greatly affect our feelings of gratitude. As we quiet our minds and let go of the cares spinning away in them, we can engage with the presence of God.

Gratitude can be as simple as acknowledging each breath we take as we focus on inhaling and exhaling. It can be attuning our attention to the light that warms our skin as the sun's rays shine on us. Stillness and gratitude are beautiful practices that go together. Spend time in silence if you can. Physically quiet your body if you cannot shut the noise out, and simply be present in the moment if possible. There's no need to rush, nowhere to go, and no tasks to worry about. Simply breathe and be here now. Give thanks for every good thing that pops into your mind.

Take five minutes by yourself without your phone. Observe what is around you or close your eyes and focus on your breathing. Thank God for the beauty of simply existing.

MORE THAN WE KNOW

Look at the sea, so big and wide,
with creatures large and small that cannot be counted.

PSALM 104:25 NCV

The world is big, and within it are more creatures, plants, and organisms than we can count. Just consider the depths of the seas and the discovery of new fish which happens regularly. What a wonderful, mysterious world we live in! When we are stuck in our own little worlds, we can't engage with the larger world where we would learn or discover something new.

One way you can practice gratitude today is by learning something new about the area where you live. You can also pick somewhere you recently traveled to if that feels more exciting. If you enjoy gardening, do some research about the pollinators in your area. If you enjoy birdwatching, look for new birds while you go for a walk outside. It can be an incredibly small act, but information is available around you to enlarge your understanding.

We can be grateful for what we already know and love, and we can also engage with gratitude by learning something new. Pick an area that interests you and look for new information about it today.

STAGES OF LIFE

Like newborn babies, long for the pure milk of the word,
so that by it you may grow in respect to salvation.

1 PETER 2:2 NASB

When we are babies, we need specific nutrients to help our bodies and brains grow. As babies grow into toddlers, they can try new foods. In short, during the different stages of life our nutrient needs are different. This is as true in our spiritual lives as it is in our physical ones.

If you have been nourished by the elemental milk of God's Word, it could feel comfortable to stay in that place. But if you don't start eating more solid food and test the Words that have been feeding you, you won't grow much. Recognizing that there are different needs at different stages can help bring freedom when we outgrow old ways. The fruit of the Spirit remains the same, so let's allow ourselves the freedom to grow as God meant us to!

Take some time to consider the stage of life you are in. What spiritual stage do you think you have entered? What might you need more or less of? With gratitude, allow yourself to make changes without any guilt or reservation about changing the way you always did things before.

POWERFUL WORDS

The tongue is a small part of the body
yet it carries great power! Just think of how a small flame
can set a huge forest ablaze.

JAMES 3:5 TPT

Our words are powerful. They can bring edification and encouragement and thereby connect us to the people around us. Or they can cause damage when we use them as weapons. The way we speak about or to ourselves is as important as how we talk to others.

Gratitude can help us soften our opinions about ourselves and others. By naming the things we are grateful for—beginning with ourselves—we create compassion, acknowledgment, and honor within our souls. It is easy to get distracted by the things we don't like, but what if we rewrote the narrative? As we reclaim our relationship with ourselves, every other relationship becomes strengthened including our relationship to God.

Take time today to name what you are thankful for about yourself. If it helps to do it through the lens of God's love for you, approach it that way!

SMALL SEEDS BIG GROWTH

"It is the smallest of all seeds, but it becomes the largest
of garden plants; it grows into a tree, and birds come and
make nests in its branches."

MATTHEW 13:32 NLT

Even the smallest seeds are full of great impact. Life has
seasons: planting, tending, and reaping. Sometimes the
gardens of our lives may seem dormant, but even in those
barren times the soil is preparing for what it will do next.
Let's embrace the season we are in, even as we plan for the
coming days.

Gratitude can help us focus on the possibilities that are
around us. Just because we don't see the growth yet doesn't
mean it's not happening underneath the obvious or the
visible. Let's keep tending to the seeds in our lives and
nurture the growth that is happening through our daily
habits of gratitude. As we do, we will see our gardens grow.

*When we plant seeds of gratitude, they are being watered
with our attention on them each day. As they grow, we
experience the fruit of gratitude in our lives. Think of an area
in which you want to grow, and plant seeds of thankfulness
there today.*

WHAT WE SOW

Whoever sows sparingly will also reap sparingly, and whoever sows generously will also reap generously.

2 CORINTHIANS 9:6 NIV

What we put our time, attention, and resources into will grow. It is imperative, then, that we be intentional about the areas we sow any seeds. This includes time spent connecting with others, what we do in our downtime, and the kinds of things we prioritize throughout each day. If we want to grow in an area, we need to put effort into it.

Gratitude helps us see the things that lighten our hearts and our loads. It helps to make a list of the people and the things we are grateful for. That allows us to clarify areas to grow in in the future. We can consider how much of our time is spent with those people or activities and what steps are needed to grow. If there is a discrepancy, it is time to become proactive about removing or adding in a purposeful way.

Take an honest look at how your time reflects your values. Plan your schedule carefully over the next week. Include timeslots for those people who are important to you and time to learn something new or to take steps toward an achievement. Limit or remove the things that don't add value to your life.

GREAT WISDOM

"As the heavens are higher than the earth,
So are My ways higher than your ways,
And My thoughts than your thoughts."

ISAIAH 55:9 NKJV

Though we may have learned a few things in this life, it is important to recognize that there is still so much more to learn. Our minds can't comprehend the greatness of the universe let alone the mind of the one who created it all. When we are willing to admit when we're wrong and to then redirect ourselves with the new information under our belt, we grow in maturity.

Consider some of the assumed truths you once took for granted. After maturing, things aren't so cut and dried. When was the last time you changed your mind about something? By God's grace, every day is an opportunity to learn, grow, and change. Gratitude has been used as a learning strategy and is a powerful tool. Students who practice gratitude are more resilient. They are more engaged with their teachers and with the subject matter. Let's not overlook the power of gratitude as we engage in life-long learning!

When you find yourself resistant to hearing other perspectives or ways of doing things, take a moment to be grateful for the ability to listen to others.

COMMIT IT TO GOD

Commit your activities to the LORD,
and your plans will be established.

PROVERBS 16:3 CSB

Gratitude can help us engage with purpose at the start of each day. Not everything we have to do in a day is exciting. We may find that we put off doing what feels overwhelming or boring. That does not mean that we cannot do the things that feel difficult to address in the moment.

Gratitude helps us to connect with our purpose. We may not want to create and stick to a budget but doing it will help us reach our financial goals. Without a plan, building a dream is nothing more than a wish. It most likely won't happen without marking the necessary steps it will take to get there. When we take time to thank God and to commit our activities to him before we begin, we set our hearts on pleasing him and trusting him for the details we cannot yet foresee. We have only to take the first step, and then each one after that, and trust him to lead us the rest of the way.

Take time before you start work or a task that you've been dreading and commit your heart and each activity to God. Then simply dive in and do it!

JULY

I will thank the LORD
because he is just;
I will sing praise to the name of
the LORD Most High.

PSALM 7:17 NLT

FIRM IDENTITY

See what kind of love the Father has given to us, that we should be called children of God; and so we are. The reason why the world does not know us is that it did not know him.

1 JOHN 3:1 ESV

One of the benefits of practicing gratitude is a higher self-esteem. If we are constantly comparing ourselves to others and endlessly competing for our place at the proverbial table, we will likely be working from a feeling of being unqualified. We may feel that we need to earn our worth in relationships, at the workplace, or in the world at large. However, when we focus on the goodness that we already have, the beauty of our personalities, and what we have to offer, we rid ourselves of the need to compete for any attention that boosts our egos. When we are sure of who we are and our inherent worth, it doesn't matter what others think because our identities are not rooted in anyone's opinion or the expectations of society.

Gratitude improves our overall outlook on life as well as the way we see ourselves. Even if this were the only benefit, which it's not, it would be a worthy practice. We are loved, we are created in the image of God, and we don't have to strive for our worth.

When you are tempted to compare yourself to others, turn your attention to your own life and what you are grateful for.

ROCK OF REFUGE

"My God is my rock.
I can run to him for safety…
The LORD saves me from those who want to harm me."

2 SAMUEL 22:3 NCV

Some days it's harder to find peace than other days. There are storms we cannot avoid and trials we cannot sidestep with simply thinking positively. However, this does not mean that rest isn't available to us in the middle of it. There is always palpable peace in God's presence.

One of the ways we can ground ourselves in peace is to remember the faithfulness of God. What he has done before, he will do again. You have lived through hard times before. This is not the end of you. You have life, breath, and hope left. You are resilient, and your God is a rock of refuge to run to. Let your soul take refuge in him when fear rises within you. He is always a safe place of peace. Hide yourself in him and take hope.

When you feel anxiety rising today, turn to the Lord in prayer. Ask him for help and protection. Take deep breaths, connect to what is true and good, and put your trust in the love that holds this universe together.

LIFT YOUR EYES

Raise your eyes on high
And see who has created these stars,
The One who brings out their multitude by number,
He calls them all by name;
Because of the greatness of His might
and the strength of His power,
Not one of them is missing.

ISAIAH 40:26 NASB

Sometimes our perspectives can shift simply by paying attention to the world around us. Gratitude helps us get out of our own heads and into a bigger worldview. It helps us reach outside of our negative biases and to see the positives that are also present. It is a powerful tool to shift our attitudes and our expectations.

If we wait to choose gratitude for when we feel thankfulness bubbling up inside of us, the truth is many of us will miss out on the benefits of its power. The practice of gratitude is like building a muscle. The more we use it, the stronger it becomes. Only we can choose whether we will incorporate it into our lives or not. Let's not wait for another day to see if it will meet us. Let's embrace it where we are at.

Look up from where you are right now and pick out five things you can see that you are grateful for. Acknowledge each and hold them in your heart for a moment.

SACRIFICIAL LOVE

"The greatest love of all is a love that sacrifices all.
And this great love is demonstrated when a person
sacrifices his life for his friends."

JOHN 15:13 TPT

The greatest love of all costs us something. It is not always easy to choose. It isn't always what we prefer. But it is worth every sacrifice and surrender. Love is the purest essence of God. There is no excuse for those of us who claim to follow Christ but choose to hate others. Love is patient and kind; it doesn't manipulate or control. It is freely given and freely received. We love because Christ first loved us. He is always our source.

Recognizing the power of love in our lives helps us choose to act in love toward others. The practice of gratitude can keep us grounded in love by reminding us of all that we have received and all that we now have. Love is not a limited resource. It is abundant, expansive, and near to each of us in this very moment. What a beautiful truth this is!

Consider the impact that all the forms of love have had on your life. As you recognize specific instances and certain relationships, give thanks for each one. As you go about your day, determine to love others well, even if it means sacrifice on your own part.

PRESENCE OVER PERFECTION

All glory to God, who is able to keep you from falling away and will bring you with great joy into his glorious presence without a single fault.

JUDE 1:24 NLT

We are not perfect people, and we never will be. We are human, and since God created us, he certainly knows it. Why do we resist our humanity so much? Why do we feel the need to cover our weaknesses when we all have that in common? God is greater than our weaknesses though he never holds it against us. It is love that led him to send Christ so that we are free in his salvation. If we chase ideals that are out of our reach, we will always be unsatisfied. But when we recognize our limits and realize that God still works within them, we will know the power of his presence over perfection.

We can live with excellence and integrity and still allow for our faults and flaws. We can release our need to control the narrative and instead show up authentically. When we are truly free, we are free to love and serve others well. We are free to be ourselves and to grow in maturity. We are free to experience joy in the presence of God and in the presence of others.

When perfectionism turns into judgment in your heart, release your idea of what should be and be willing to accept what is. There is good here. Can you see it?

GRATITUDE'S RETURNS

Everyone who competes in the games goes into strict training. They do it to get a crown that will not last, but we do it to get a crown that will last forever.

1 CORINTHIANS 9:25 NIV

Choosing to look on the brighter side of things doesn't take a lot of change in our daily lives. However, the effort can shift our perspectives and our attitudes drastically. We can change our perceptions anywhere without the need to spend a dime. The return for such little investment is remarkable. It is an accessible way to find more meaning in life, more satisfaction, and greater motivation to share what we have with others.

The greatest effects of gratitude come from practicing it regularly. It means choosing to see the benefit of what we already have rather than envy what we don't. It does take intentionality and a willingness to see things from a different perspective. However, even the smallest changes can have a snowball effect as they build larger patterns into our lives.

Instead of trying to overhaul your life, consider which small steps of gratitude have had the most impact this year so far. Simply being attentive to the benefits can help you choose it more throughout your day.

SURROUNDED BY PEACE

"Is not the LORD your God with you? And has He not given you rest on every side? For He has given the inhabitants of the land into my hand, and the land is subdued before the LORD and before His people."

1 CHRONICLES 22:18 NKJV

There are many Scriptures that speak of the rest that God offers us. Psalm 23 is a beautiful example of how God leads us into the refreshing rest of his presence. He watches over our souls, guiding us to places where we can be restored. He put rhythms of repose into place at the beginning starting with the establishment of the Sabbath. Rest is powerful, and we should not ignore the necessity to incorporate it into our lives.

In a society which never seems to slow down, it can feel as if we are breaking the rules by prioritizing rest. We were not created for a constant hustle, though. We were created to embrace the cycles and the seasons and to live by them. This includes making regular rest a priority in our lives. We need to work, yes, and gratitude helps balance the pressure to produce with the truth that we don't have to strive for our worth. There is rest available today on every side.

Pick a day each week to truly rest, whatever restfulness looks like for you. Find whatever it is that refreshes, restores, and fills you. Don't do any work that you don't want to on that day.

SEEING THINGS RIGHTLY

The next day John saw Jesus coming toward him and said,
"Look, the Lamb of God, who takes away
the sin of the world!"

JOHN 1:29 CSB

One interesting way our brains are wired is to recognize threats around us. It is easy to become overwhelmed by the negativity in our lives because we are prone to see it as a threat to our well-being. Even though this is natural, it does not mean we are powerless in our thinking or our reactions.

The practice of gratitude connects us to the goodness that is already here. If we look for reasons to be thankful, we will find them. Nothing is too insignificant that it cannot be counted in our blessings. Nothing is too grandiose that we shouldn't celebrate it for its beauty. Gratitude helps us balance the hard aspects of life so that we see things more clearly. Not everything in life is a trial or a test, and not everything in life is wonderful. There are numerous experiences to be lived through, but we can practice gratitude in every season and each situation.

Learning the power of acceptance can help us connect to gratitude in every situation. We cannot tell what tomorrow will hold, but we can be thankful for what we have today. Practice accepting what is before you before you choose how you will move forward.

GRATITUDE AND BELIEF

"Whatever you ask in prayer,
believe that you have received it,
and it will be yours."

MARK 11:24 ESV

Gratitude can greatly affect the way you see things. It can influence your expectations, as well as your outlook. If we feel powerless in our lives, we may find ourselves becoming resentful. When we recognize, however, that we have agency over our lives, gratitude is inherent in our ability to choose.

We are not bound to others' expectations of us. We get to choose at every point how we want to exist in this world. Gratitude as a practice helps us take ownership of our thoughts, and in turn, it can help us make choices that reflect our values rather than the opinions of those around us. Gratitude helps us connect to what truly matters in life and to us. This is a gift that cannot be overstated!

When you feel boxed in by someone, remember that you can choose your actions and reactions. Choose how you want to participate. Consider your thoughts about God and his intentions for you. Do you believe that he is good? Do you believe that he is wise? Use prayer as a building block in your relationship with him.

A WORTHWHILE WAIT

Our homeland is in heaven, and we are waiting for our
Savior, the Lord Jesus Christ, to come from heaven.

PHILIPPIANS 3:20 NCV

Gratitude is extremely helpful in creating resilience and
improving patience in those who practice it. It is important
that we keep the element of novelty in our gratitude
practices so that they don't become stale. If we list the same
three things which we are grateful for repeatedly, we lose
out on one of the most important parts of the practice—
something new and positive to focus on.

As we practice looking for new reasons to be grateful, our
brains become accustomed to searching them out. We won't
have to resort to the same reasons, though we may want to
revisit them, and that's okay! Our minds, though, will look
for fresh ones we may not have noticed yesterday. This very
practice roots us in the present as we connect to the unique
goodness in our experiences. Then waiting is not only more
bearable; it becomes enjoyable.

*Take one of your recent positive experiences and write out all
the details you can remember about it.*

THE JOYS OF TODAY

This is the day which the LORD has made;
Let's rejoice and be glad in it.

PSALM 118:24 NASB

As we engage with the joys that today offers, we give ourselves the gift of mindfulness, presence, and connection to this moment. There are many forms the goodness can take: a quiet morning, a smile exchanged with a stranger, a child's laughter, your own light-heartedness. Whatever brings lightness and life is a joy to be embraced!

Let's focus our attention on the day as it unfolds, not on the nebulous happiness of another time or place. Joy can be found in the details of our day. It can be found here even now. As we put our intentions into looking for reasons to rejoice, we will find them. Even the smallest joys are buoyancy for hope.

Be intentional about looking for little joys throughout your day. With each one, treasure them in your heart, and thank God that you have so many reasons to rejoice in the day he has given you.

HEALING OINTMENT

He heals the wounds of every shattered heart.

PSALM 147:3 TPT

For those who practice gratitude, studies show that there is a boost to their overall well-being. Stress levels go down, sleep patterns can improve, and resilience is strengthened. We cannot escape heartbreak in this life, but we can move through it with hope, knowing the pain won't last forever. Gratitude can help ground us in the goodness of life, even as we experience the harder parts of it.

Though we cannot avoid the painful parts of life no matter how much we hope to, we can know the goodness of God in the middle of them. He is our peace in the storm, our joy in the mundane, and our landing spot when we feel windswept by the gales of change. God's love heals wounds and binds up the broken-hearted. Gratitude helps us remember that healing is possible, for we have not been abandoned in our trouble. We are embraced by love throughout it all.

Gratitude has been shown to lessen aches and pains. When you are hurting, turn your attention to what you are grateful for, and keep going!

GRACIOUS FREEDOM

Sin is no longer your master,
for you no longer live under the requirements of the law.
Instead, you live under the freedom of God's grace.

ROMANS 6:14 NLT

Gratitude connects us to the reality and truth of goodness wherever we are in this moment. One of the most liberating truths in Scripture is that Christ has set us completely free with his grace. We are not bound to our sin or to any of our failures; we are liberated by the gracious mercy of his heart. We get to choose how to use this freedom, so why not use it to be grateful?

Mindfulness is an important part of practicing gratitude. Mindfulness is defined by the Oxford dictionary as the quality or state of being conscious or aware of something. To live mindfully means to live in a state of consciousness and to be connected to the moment as it happens. Gratitude helps us turn our awareness to the good things in our lives and in this world. There is freedom to engage in it anytime, anywhere. We are not slaves to our impulses or our thoughts; we can train our minds to see things differently!

When negative, intrusive thoughts pop up, choose to assert yourself over them. Ground yourself in the present by naming three things that are true and good right now.

FOCUS

I do not run like someone running aimlessly;
I do not fight like a boxer beating the air.

1 CORINTHIANS 9:26 NIV

In an age of instant gratification where so much information is readily accessible, it can be difficult to train ourselves to focus on one thing at a time. Many of us struggle to quell diverting interests, but there are times when our undivided attention is needed. When having a conversation with someone, when trying to move ahead on a work project, or when doing an important task, focus is needed.

The practice of gratitude helps set our thoughts in a specific direction. We are not slaves to our thoughts, or at least it certainly shouldn't feel like it is. Thoughts come and go, and they don't all hold the same weight. When we focus on one thing, even for only short bursts at a time, it strengthens our ability to accomplish our work. This way, we can make headway in the direction we want to go, not as someone who runs aimlessly and is pulled by distractions along the way.

Set a timer for five minutes and think of all the things you are grateful for. You pray as well, but don't get caught up in any to-dos. The time to focus on that will come. Try to do one thing at a time today.

POWERFUL PEACE

The peace of God, which surpasses all understanding,
will guard your hearts and minds through Christ Jesus.

PHILIPPIANS 4:7 NKJV

The practice of gratitude can turn a bad day into a good
one, all by the power of perspective. We may not be able
to change what happens to us, but we can change how we
think about it. That, my friend, is an invitation to peace.
When we feel empowered by the ability to choose our
reactions, we already have access to the peace of God that
surpasses all understanding. The point is this: we don't need
understanding to experience peace. And we don't have to
rationalize things in order to be grateful for them.

As we join our practices with God's presence, we experience
his peace which settles our hearts and our minds. We don't
have to worry about tomorrow. We can look for reasons to
be grateful today. Every small thing matters. Every shift in
perspective is a victory.

*When something frustrating happens today, look for a reason
to be thankful in whatever the solution ends up being.*

KEEP GOING

Just as you have received Christ Jesus as Lord,
continue to walk in him.

COLOSSIANS 2:6 CSB

Gratitude should not be a one-time action. Instead, it is
the continuous habit of it that produces the most impact in
our lives. This isn't hyperbole; this is what science shows us
is true. The benefits of gratitude come with incorporating
it into our lives in consistent ways. The more gratitude we
express, the more grateful we become. This may sound
simplistic, but it is nonetheless true.

Consistency builds pathways to success, and this is as true
with our neural pathways as with our physical efforts.
When we make a practice of gratitude, we strengthen
the part of our brain that looks for reasons to be grateful.
This is beneficial, not only to our mental health, but to
every area of our lives. This practice gives our mental and
physical efforts deep satisfaction as we experience each
positive moment.

*If you haven't already done so, schedule a time to incorporate
your gratitude practice. Try for the same time each day so
the habit is easier to build! Write it in your calendar if that
helps and set a reminder.*

VICTORIOUS MINDSETS

Thanks be to God, who gives us the victory
through our Lord Jesus Christ.

1 CORINTHIANS 15:57 ESV

Have you ever been around someone who could not seem
to think of a good thing going on in their life? Perhaps their
negativity is situational, or it seems to be a permanent part
of their personality. Part of this may be due to an innate
negativity bias. Negativity bias is a cognitive bias that makes
a person more drawn to things of a negative nature, or it
seems to have a greater effect on their psychological state.
Though negativity bias is a real thing to contend with, we
can create new pathways to combatting it with a consistent
connection to gratitude.

Gratitude helps us see goodness in the world rather than
just focusing on the negative aspects of it. It brings balance
to our perspectives, and it helps us look for more of the
positives as we practice it. Our identities do not consist
merely of the thoughts we think, but we can certainly think
better thoughts by intentionally looking outside our own
perspectives.

What are the most meaningful things and people in your life?
Focus on them today and connect with them in tangible ways.

EXPRESSIONS OF GRATITUDE

"You should be a light for other people.
Live so that they will see the good things you do
and will praise your Father in heaven."

MATTHEW 5:16 NCV

Research supports the idea that expressing gratitude can strengthen our relationships. It is a good practice to thank people for the things they do that we appreciate. This is common courtesy. Going beyond this, we can also express gratitude in other ways. We can look for creative ways to go beyond a simple "thank you." Our connections are strengthened through gratitude, especially when it starts with what we think about others.

We certainly don't have to keep score of what others have done for us or what we do for them, but being aware of our blessings initiated by others can help us to find a starting place and motivate us to return favors in kind. Did a friend buy you a meal? Consider doing the same for them next opportunity you have. Going beyond this, you can write letters, send a quick text that tells them what you appreciate about them, or give them undistracted time to talk. Gratitude begets gratitude. Don't shy away from sharing the love!

Be intentional about expressing gratitude in the interactions you have with others throughout the day.

CONSIDER IT

"Only fear the LORD and serve Him in truth with all your heart; for consider what great things He has done for you."

1 SAMUEL 12:24 NASB

Gratitude is the natural result of considering the positive aspects of life around us. It is an expression of thankfulness that can be communicated for just about anything. When we practice it regularly it can benefit our mental, physical, emotional, and spiritual health. It can strengthen our relationships and give us a deeper sense of purpose.

Take time to consider the goodness you have experienced in your life. It can be encouraging to realize that you are living such blessings that you couldn't have dreamed them in your younger years. What goodness is now in your life that you didn't know to hope for before? Consider it and give thanks for the wonder of your present blessings.

Pick an area of your life where you are experiencing satisfaction and think through the last several years. Are you surprised by the goodness of your reality as opposed to what you expected in your life to play out? Be specific about what you are grateful for.

AWE-INDUCING BEAUTY

God, you are so resplendent and radiant!
Your majesty shines from your everlasting mountain.
Nothing could be compared to you in glory!

PSALM 76:4 TPT

Engaging in activities that awaken awe in our hearts is
a worthwhile endeavor. The sensation of awe is quite
powerful. It sends shivers down our spines, makes us feel
warm in our chests, and makes it feel as if time slows down.
Everything about the moment feels poignant—holy, even.

Think about the last time you experienced awe in a visceral
way. Where were you? What were you doing? Allow yourself
to engage in that moment all over again as you bring it to
mind. Perhaps you feel the sensation even now as you think
about it. This feeling of awe can be found in the presence of
God, and it can be experienced anywhere you are.

*Recall a time that you were overcome with awe and wonder.
Share that memory with someone today.*

OPPORTUNITIES FOR REST

"Come to me, all of you who are weary and carry heavy burdens, and I will give you rest."

MATTHEW 11:28 NLT

We can be weighed down by the burdens of life if we do not offer them to God. Gratitude reminds us that our hearts are lightened with God's love, and yet it's a continual invitation to unburden ourselves in him. We can have his presence now and accept his growing influence over our burdens.

When we spend time in prayer and offer up to God all that is weighing us down, we free ourselves to rest in his presence. He takes the weight that is not for us to carry on our own. We don't have to struggle under those wearying burdens by ourselves any longer. As we give to him all that is his, we can free ourselves to follow up with our gratitude practices. What a powerful dynamic this can be for our rest in our minds, bodies, and souls!

Before you do your gratitude practice today, take a few minutes to offer to the Lord in prayer all that is burdening your mind and your heart.

TELL THEM

"May the LORD repay you for what you have done. May you be richly rewarded by the LORD, the God of Israel, under whose wings you have come to take refuge."

RUTH 2:12 NIV

Gratitude is a gift that keeps on giving. Just think of random acts of kindness that have inspired others to pay it forward in the same measure. When we express gratitude to others, it doesn't stop with us. Even if you never know the impact of your words, share them generously regardless.

Sometimes we can be swift to offer criticism but we're slow with our appreciation. What if we flip that script? Why not readily share the gratitude we have for others and only ever slowly criticize them? When we do, our relationships are strengthened. Think back to a time when someone expressed their heartfelt thanks to you. How did it make you feel? Endeavor to make someone else feel that way today!

When someone does something kind for you today, express your gratitude generously.

PERFECT PORTION

My flesh and my heart fail;
But God is the strength of my heart and my portion forever.

PSALM 73:26 NKJV

Gratitude helps us focus on what we have now rather than the lack we may feel as we look ahead. We cannot tell what tomorrow will bring in either joy or sorrow, but we can ground ourselves in the goodness of God which is with us now. The presence of the Spirit is our strength and there is grace to rest in his peace in this moment.

God provided manna in the desert every day for forty years for his people. He offered them their daily portion, their daily bread, just as Jesus teaches us to pray. He will not leave us without our needs met. Are there moments when we feel acutely needy? Of course, but gratitude can help direct us to the faithfulness of God and the abundance of his love which provides our portion today. He has not failed us yet, and he never will.

When you feel worried about provision in the future, allow yourself to look at where you are today. Where is there enough? Where is there more than enough? Give thanks for what you uncover, and trust God with the rest.

INNER RENEWAL

We do not give up. Even though our outer person is being destroyed, our inner person is being renewed day by day.

2 CORINTHIANS 4:16 CSB

Living with intentional thankfulness is like a wellspring of renewal in our inner beings. The continual, daily practice of gratitude changes the patterns in our brains. A thankful attitude is not reserved for those living with immense amounts of privilege. It is an approach that we can incorporate no matter who we are, what our circumstances are, or where we are in any moment.

Gratitude is a choice to engage with the goodness available to us now, and to trust that when we look for beauty, we will find it. All it takes to experience this is to practice it! Thankful hearts renew our minds and make us more resilient in the face of hardship. During the storms we can recognize the gifts of life that are still with us. Gratitude leads to renewal, which leads to more gratitude. It is a beautiful loop that benefits our whole beings.

Connect to three things that are refreshing in your life today, even if that connection is simply the acknowledgment of the gift and gratitude for it.

HEALTHY OUTLOOK

The light of the eyes rejoices the heart,
and good news refreshes the bones.

PROVERBS 15:30 ESV

Gratitude is not only a practice that benefits your outlook on life. It is also good for your physical health. Just as the best benefits of an exercise routine happen with regular movement, the same is true of your gratitude practice. Even just taking a few minutes a day to focus on it can benefit your body in ways you may not have even thought about.

It is well known in the health community that behavior is directly linked to biology. We can change our health by changing our behavior. This works both ways—negative and positive. Gratitude is a practice that benefits us in almost every way. Numerous studies have shown that there is a direct link between gratitude and our aches and pains, inflammation, and sleep quality. Gratitude is not only good for our minds; it is also good for our bodies.

Spend some time being thankful for what your body has done and continues to do for you. Put a hand over the parts that stand out to you and release gratitude as you thank God specifically for your body.

DIFFERENT REPRESENTATIONS

There are different kinds of gifts,
but they are all from the same Spirit.

1 CORINTHIANS 12:4 NCV

When we learn to delight in our unique personalities, our different ways of thinking, and our gifts, we embrace who we are created to be. Comparisons can lead us to think less of ourselves. Gratitude can help us to be grounded in the beauty of who we are and live confidently from that place.

Our identity is not in what others think of us but instead is found in our inherent worth. We were each created in the image of a marvelous and creative God. He doesn't make mistakes. He delights in the diversity of his creation, and we should too. Gratitude can help us by giving us eyes to see difference as beautiful, not as a threat. The Spirit is the same, and his fruit is clear, even if our expressions look different. Gratitude is shown to increase self-esteem as each of us recognize the beauty of who we individually are. This is a beautiful and holy thing!

When you are tempted to judge either yourself or someone else because of your differences, look for the beauty within those variations. Name three things that you can be grateful for in these differences.

HEARTFELT AFFECTIONS

"Where your treasure is,
there your heart will be also."

MATTHEW 6:21 NASB

What we treasure, there our hearts will be. If we are consumed by our status, our hearts will be preoccupied with how we can achieve our own glory. We will value people who have a higher status while neglecting those who don't have a lot of value in society. Gratitude helps us connect with the goodness of God in every sector of social life. When we treasure the values of God's kingdom, our hearts will be filled with those attributes.

Practicing gratitude helps us be more gracious to others. We are more apt to give the benefit of the doubt rather than jumping to harsh conclusions. We are more likely to be led by compassion in our choices. Gratitude helps keep our values rooted in what really matters to God. Instead of getting caught up in the cycle of valuing meaningless things which quickly fade, we can remain grounded in the beauty, goodness, and hope around us.

Soul satisfaction is increased through the practice of gratitude. Meditate on an area of life that you perhaps have struggled with, but which now seems much lighter and easier. Thank God for the ease you now experience.

GREATER THAN GOLD

These only reveal the sterling core of your faith, which is far more valuable than gold that perishes, for even gold is refined by fire. Your authentic faith will result in even more praise, glory, and honor when Jesus the Anointed One is revealed.

1 PETER 1:7 TPT

There are things in this life that are more valuable than any wealth. Jesus was clear when he said that love is the highest goal; it is the fulfillment of the law and the prophets. Love covers everything we are meant to adhere to. It is both the source and the desire.

Gratitude helps us grow in faith as we taste and see the goodness of God in the details of our lives. Bonds of trust are strengthened as we focus on the faithful love of God revealed in the beauty of each delight and provision. We can find reasons to give gratitude in many areas: in our relationships, in the beauty of the natural world, and in our sense of awe when we witness the synergy of God's plan for us. May we prioritize the continuation of practicing gratitude, especially in the hard times for there are treasures to be found in the darkness if we are willing to look for them.

In hindsight, where can you see gifts of goodness that were hard to recognize during a hard time in your life?

ENRICHED IN EVERY WAY

You will be enriched in every way so that you can always be generous. And when we take your gifts to those who need them, they will thank God.

2 CORINTHIANS 9:11 NLT

Generosity is a practical side effect of incorporating gratitude into our lives. When we recognize the abundance, or even the sufficiency, of what we have in this moment, we can readily recognize what we have which we can share with others. A feeling of want will leave us resistant to being generous but knowing that we have all we need leads us to share openly and willingly with others.

Though gratitude is often inwardly focused, it does not end there. We are filled up so we may pour out. We are enriched in every way so we can be generous, as Paul said in today's verse. Research shows that gratitude acts as a primer for generosity. It has been observed that grateful people give more. In the end, everyone benefits from our practice of gratitude.

After spending time connecting to what you are grateful for today, consider how you can sow into others in practical ways. Follow through on your intentions.

LET IT GO

Get rid of all bitterness, rage and anger, brawling and slander, along with every form of malice.

EPHESIANS 4:31 NIV

When we focus on bitter feelings, offenses, and hatred, intensity for those emotions seems to grow. We should not demean ourselves when we have reactive feelings, but we also shouldn't ignore them. As we observe our own reactions, we make room for self-compassion just as we would when we observe the reactions of other people. However, this is just the starting point.

If we want to build cycles of support in our hearts and minds, gratitude is a wonderful way to do so. Focusing only on the negatives will leave us feeling frustrated and powerless. Focusing on what we have to be grateful for shifts the narrative and balances out the heavy things in life with the lighter ones. If you want to let go of bitterness, anger, slander, and the like, incorporate a practice of gratitude to aid you in it.

Pinpoint a frustration that makes you feel bitterness or anger. Come up with at least one thing that could counteract that thought with the opposite effect. If you struggle with someone's lack of communication, for instance, perhaps you can be thankful that you are able to communicate at least a small bit regardless.

SHARED BLESSINGS

"The Lord bless you and keep you;
The Lord make His face shine upon you,
And be gracious to you;
The Lord lift up His countenance upon you,
And give you peace."

Numbers 6:24–26 NKJV

Today's verse is a benediction, which is a prayer or blessing which promotes well-being. In the overflow of our gratitude, we can bless others and pray for their awakened understanding of goodness, peace, and grace available from God. Blessings were a common practice in the Scriptures. Benedictions are also known in some Christian traditions today. The power of sharing a blessing can be used in our personal lives as well.

You don't have to get creative with your benedictions if you aren't inspired to do so. You can use ones found in Scripture and adopt them for your own personal use. Today's verse is a good example. It is a practical way to ask for God's divine favor to rest on others. We can join with the heart of God to see the goodness already available.

Even if you only do it in your heart and mind, release a benediction and a blessing over someone today, especially if you see someone struggling.

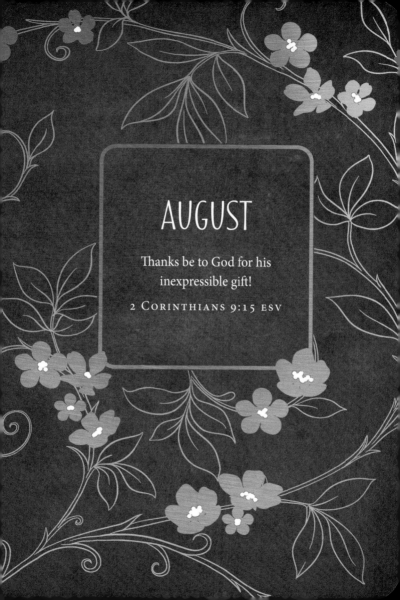

AUGUST

Thanks be to God for his
inexpressible gift!

2 Corinthians 9:15 esv

GOOD FRUIT

The fruit of the Spirit is love, joy, peace, patience, kindness, goodness, faithfulness, gentleness, and self-control. The law is not against such things.

GALATIANS 5:22-23 CSB

The fruits of the Spirit are the attributes by which we should measure the quality of our lives. It's not about how much money we have, the size of our families, or the address of our homes or businesses. Can we find reasons to be grateful with each of these blessings? Of course. But are they the qualifiers of our life satisfaction? Not by any means.

Spirit-fruit is the evidence of God's kingdom at work in us. Love, joy, peace, patience, kindness, goodness, faithfulness, gentleness, and self-control are the evidence of goodness in our lives and as we minister to others in this world. If we are having trouble looking for the good, let's look for these qualities in ourselves. As we seek them, we will find them. And when we find them, we know that the Spirit is at work in our souls.

Thank God for every expression of these attributes of his kingdom that you find in or around you today.

GREATEST MEASURE

"You shall love the LORD your God with all your heart and with all your soul and with all your strength and with all your mind, and your neighbor as yourself."

LUKE 10:27 ESV

The greatest commandment isn't to know the Bible through and through. It's not to show up to church multiple times a week. It's not in our own perfection—not at all! The greatest commandment is to love God with our whole beings and to love those around us. We don't get to choose who our neighbors are; we simply get to treat others the same way we would want to be treated.

The practice of gratitude not only helps us connect to the goodness present in our lives, but it can also help us treat others better. When we recognize the ways in which we are loved, we can engage more freely with others by treating them with kindness and respect. Gratitude doesn't alienate us from others; it makes us see the ways in which we are connected.

Think of the simplest areas of your life and what you are grateful for about them. Consider the things which you have no control over. As you give thanks, remember to let that gratitude guide you in your interactions with others today.

VISIBLE TRANSFORMATIONS

Our faces, then, are not covered. We all show the Lord's glory, and we are being changed to be like him. This change in us brings ever greater glory, which comes from the Lord, who is the Spirit.

2 CORINTHIANS 3:18 NCV

In the Old Testament, Moses encountered God's glory. Afterwards, his face shown with the glory of God and reflected that he had been in his presence. As we spend time in God's presence, we are transformed into his image. In the same way, the more time we spend expressing gratitude, the more grateful we become.

Even those of us who tend toward being morose can experience hope with this practice. The more we choose to practice gratitude, the more we will look for reasons to be grateful. New neural pathways are created, and our outlooks become brighter as we reflect on the goodness that is present in our lives. We won't be able to hide our perspectives from others; people around us will see the effects of gratitude's power as it plays out in our more positive perspectives.

Don't give up practicing gratitude if it feels challenging today. Find a fresh way to engage with it instead. Take a picture of something that catches your eye and come back to it at the end of the day.

FOCUS IN

Let your eyes look directly ahead
And let your gaze be fixed straight in front of you.

PROVERBS 4:25 NASB

Too often we miss out on the goodness right here and now because we are fixated on what we don't have. Instead of taking these blessings for granted, gratitude helps us appreciate them. As we grow in appreciation, we will project it to the people in our lives.

It is important that we remain intentional with our perspectives and our intentions. We cannot control every thought that comes into our minds. We are not meant to. Instead of judging ourselves for habits or conditioning, let's do the work necessary to build new ones. Practicing gratitude helps us redirect our thoughts and choose our reactions. When we remain focused on what matters and on the beauty that we are living in, we can strengthen our connections by expressing the appreciation in our hearts.

Pick one area of beauty or goodness such as a good relationship or a solid job and determine to give thanks for it in various ways today.

TENDER DEVOTION

Be devoted to tenderly loving your fellow believers as members of one family. Try to outdo yourselves in respect and honor of one another.

ROMANS 12:10 TPT

Love is beautifully expressed through our devotion. For example, a devoted spouse remains faithful to their partner and expresses loyalty and enthusiasm for them. Our love can always grow in fresh ways, allowing our loved ones to truly feel appreciated. This is where gratitude can play a powerful part in our relationships.

What would our relationships look like if we tried to outdo one another with respect and honor for each other? What if we lavished our love on each other, vocally sharing our appreciation for one another? By putting intention behind our expressions of love, rather than simply taking each other for granted, we can grow in trust, love, and gratitude. What a beautiful world this would be if we all endeavored to live this way.

Go out of your way to show appreciation for those closest to you in your life. Stretch yourself to go beyond what you would normally do or say. Be extravagant!

IT'S POSSIBLE

I can do everything through Christ,
who gives me strength.

PHILIPPIANS 4:13 NLT

When we feel powerless, we can also feel stuck. When we feel stuck, we may struggle to know what our choices are. Gratitude can shift our perspectives such that we don't only see the hard things in life, but also the life-giving aspects. As we practice thankfulness, we take ownership of our minds and allow ourselves to see alternatives to the uncomfortable aspects of life. We may not be able to dictate what we face in life, but we can manage our reactions.

Christ helps us in our hardships, and his strength meets us in our weaknesses. There is power in his presence to overcome and press through. Gratitude helps us develop perseverance in that a more positive perspective reminds us that it is not all hard. It is not all impossible. Life is not only made up of obstacles. There are a million little gifts all around us when we start to see them, and they bring relief, peace, and joy.

As you go through your day, make a running list in your phone or somewhere that you can easily access of all the beauty you find.

WHAT IT'S ALL FOR

For the joy set before him he endured the cross, scorning its shame, and sat down at the right hand of the throne of God.

HEBREWS 12:2 NIV

Gratitude can help us connect to our deeply held values. When we practice harmonizing our attentions to what we are thankful for, one of the benefits is that we appreciate what is already in our lives. We don't have to strive to attain it, but rather it clarifies that which matters greatly to us.

Gratitude is such a simple practice, but it yields great returns. We can experience more pleasure and joy just by incorporating gratitude practices in our lives. Studies show that people who make a concerted effort to incorporate thankfulness into their routines experience higher levels of positive emotions, l more optimism, and are more connected to their lives. If we want to throw off the things that hinder us, seeking to find gratitude is an important and simple way to do it!

Begin and end your day with gratitude, noting a few things that you are thankful for today.

STAY HUMBLE

Be of the same mind toward one another. Do not set your mind on high things, but associate with the humble. Do not be wise in your own opinion.

ROMANS 12:16 NKJV

There is no class system in the kingdom of God. All people are loved and worthy of time, attention, and grace. Each person is valued. Let's resist the urge to put some people on pedestals while overlooking others. Gratitude can help us see the value in those we might otherwise take for granted.

Even the practice of gratitude is a humble one. There are no entry requirements. Anyone can practice gratitude wherever they are in the world. They don't need to have anything more or to become anyone else. Gratitude is accessible and free to all. When we practice it, we not only look for the goodness around us, but we also endeavor to see the positives in people. Gratitude helps us remain humble and open to others by focusing our attention on the beauty that lies within them.

If you find yourself having a hard time with someone today, offer the benefit of the doubt while picking out one thing about them you can genuinely be thankful for.

CAPTIVATED THOUGHTS

We demolish arguments and every proud thing that is raised up against the knowledge of God, and we take every thought captive to obey Christ.

2 CORINTHIANS 10:4-5 CSB

Gratitude helps us redirect our thoughts and connect to what is already present and good in our lives. When we feel overwhelmed, it may not feel natural to look for the good. However, the more we practice gratitude in both good and bad times, the more we reap the benefits of it.

There are many ways we can engage in gratitude daily. We can take time to observe all that is going on around us and acknowledge whatever stands out most to us. We can keep gratitude journals and recount good things that happened, beautiful people we encountered, or something unique that we observed that day. The practice of gratitude is an act of turning our thoughts. It's the making of an effort to direct our thinking so we become grounded in the goodness which is already accessible to us. As we do this, we train our minds to do it more and more.

Instead of engaging in arguments that are typically fed by pride, let's take some time to cool down. As we do, we can become more grounded in the moment. It might help to name three things that are true and life-giving right now.

SPRINGS OF LIFE

Keep your heart with all vigilance,
for from it flow the springs of life.

PROVERBS 4:23 ESV

Our hearts contain what we value, what we hope for, and the core of who we are. What we love is embraced within our hearts. We are whole people—body and spirit—and our hearts are a crucial part of those.

What does today's verse mean when it says we should keep our hearts with all vigilance? The Hebrew word used for heart in this case is *levav*. The word includes our thoughts, our wills, our affections, and our discernment. Gratitude helps us guard all these things by turning our attentions to what is good, true, valuable, and beautiful. If we are intentional about our thinking, we safeguard the springs of life that flow from our hearts. We experience deeper satisfaction in our lives and our relationships, and we think more positively about the future. What an important tool gratitude is in keeping us aligned with the Lord's love!

What are the three most important things in your life? How much time do you spend thinking about them and supporting them? Evaluate whether you would rather focus more on those special items today.

CONTINUE IN THIS WAY

Continue praying, keeping alert,
and always thanking God.

COLOSSIANS 4:2 NCV

Practice takes consistent effort. Practice doesn't have to mean spending hours each day on something. It can be as simple as focusing a few regular and minutes each day. In order to see the most benefits, consistency is imperative.

New beginnings are exciting and have with them an innate motivation. However, repetition can make our practices feel stale if we are not looking for new ways, different exercises, or fresh activities to keep them feeling alive. We can continue to practice gratitude and still look for new ways to express it. We can take a walk rather than sit in our favorite chair. We can sing what we are thankful for rather than make a list. Whatever makes us feel connected to it is what's important. Let's not limit ourselves to the same strategies. The important thing is that we continue!

Try a new way of expressing your gratitude today, whether it's through song, dance, art, conversations, or walks. Find a way to do whatever feels fresh in your soul.

BELIEVE AND DECLARE

I certainly believed that I would see
the goodness of the LORD
In the land of the living.

PSALM 27:13 NASB

Psalm 27 is David's song of poetic praise to God before he was anointed king over Israel. Even in his anxiousness, David believed that he would see the goodness of God throughout his life. David had already experienced God's help in many ways, and perhaps it was these experiences that gave him faith to hope for breakthroughs again.

In times of trouble, it can be difficult to connect to peace, but when we remember what we have already lived through, we can find grace to believe there will be better days ahead. Our faith is bolstered when we reflect on the faithfulness of God toward us. We don't have to blindly believe; we look at the goodness that is already here, and we can strengthen our trust in God as we look to the future.

Whether you are having a good day or a bad day, you can find goodness to connect to. Spend time engaging in an activity that makes you grateful. Talk to a friend, walk a pet, or watch the sunset as you mindfully engage with a blessing. Thank God that there is more goodness ahead in the unknown future.

CHOOSE KINDNESS

Be kind and affectionate toward one another. Has God
graciously forgiven you? Then graciously forgive one
another in the depths of Christ's love.

EPHESIANS 4:32 TPT

When we appreciate what we have received, we can extend
our gratitude in practical acts of kindness. When we have
been forgiven, it is only right that we offer the same grace to
others. This is reminiscent of the parable of the unmerciful
servant in Matthew 18. His great debt was forgiven by his
master, and he was freed from it, but then he turned around
and pressured another man who owed him even less for
restitution. The gracious thing to do out of his gratitude
would have been to also forgive his own debtor.

Gratitude for what we have been given connects us to a
deeper sense of generosity. Perhaps if that servant had
taken time to reflect on the relief and deep gratitude he felt
for his forgiven debt, he might have chosen to act in kind.
In any case, gratitude helps us remember the generosity
we have been shown. We choose what we do with the
generosity and kindness extended to us, but it's God's will
that it increases our desire to be generous with others.

*Reflect on a time when you were given something that gave
you great relief. How did it make you feel then, and how do
you feel now? Consider paying it forward to someone else.*

ACTIVE PARTICIPATION

Put on your new nature, created to be like God-truly righteous and holy.

EPHESIANS 4:24 NLT

Our thinking is not transformed for the better by accident. Personal growth is not guaranteed to us. We must put some effort into the objective in order to achieve it. In today's verse, Paul says, "Put on your new nature." This new nature is found in Christ, but it is something in which we must actively participate. Gratitude is a great way to remember the important things in life, to connect to deeper meaning, and to take ownership of the direction of our attentions.

We don't strive to receive God's love. He freely gives it. However, we still act to receive it. We open our hearts to him, and he fills us with the power of his presence. He will not bypass our permission. We must make room and act upon the invitation we have been given. It is simple, but it still requires agency on our part. The benefits of gratitude are found in the consistent participation of it. Let's not forget that our choices matter, and they affect how we live.

Choose how you want to treat others today with intention. Give gratitude for the ability to participate in your life. You are the driver, not a passenger!

POWER TO OVERCOME

You, dear children, are from God and have overcome them, because the one who is in you is greater than the one who is in the world.

1 JOHN 4:4 NIV

Gratitude helps us tune into the presence of God. It helps to open our senses to the grace that is in our midst already. There is strength in knowing what is available to us. As we let go of our anxieties about the unknown, we can draw courage from what we know to be true here and now.

Gratitude is not an escape hatch from our problems. It does, however, help us build resilience because it draws our attention to what is good, right, and beautiful. As we practice thankfulness, our resources for patience and resilience grow. We can truly find the power to overcome every hindrance with the presence of Christ as we turn our attentions to him repeatedly.

Take some time to think about the resources you have available to you now—your home, your friends, and your family. When you feel overwhelmed, be grounded in what is already yours today.

GRATITUDE BUILDS TRUST

The LORD is good,
A stronghold in the day of trouble;
And He knows those who trust in Him.

NAHUM 1:7 NKJV

When we express appreciation to those around us, trust is built. Research shows that the positive emotions we experience when someone expresses gratitude build stronger connections between us. To be sure, trust is also built with connection and follow through, but it is very powerful when people feel seen and appreciated for who they are and what they are already doing.

We shouldn't take this simple tool for granted in building stronger relationships. Gratitude is a powerful practice in our own lives which influences our health in all sorts of ways. And its effects don't stop there. If we want stronger relationships, expressing appreciation is a powerful way to build that! Consider the last time someone genuinely thanked you for something you did for them. How did it make you feel? When we feel respected, our natural reaction is to trust that relationship more.

Be intentional about expressing appreciation to the people in your life today.

WISE BUILDERS

"Everyone who hears these words of mine and acts on them will be like a wise man who built his house on the rock."

MATTHEW 7:24 CSB

With our intentions and actions, we build our lives. We cannot tell what kinds of weather will storm throughout our lives, but we can focus on building a strong foundation that won't easily give way under pressure. Gratitude is a helpful perspective which opens our eyes to the important things in life. When we know what to focus on, we will give our energy to it without wasting time or energy on what we cannot control.

When we follow the Word of the Lord, we choose wisely. Let's not ignore, then, the encouragement to enter his courts with thanksgiving and his house with praise. Let's not forget to encourage each other and treat one another the way we want to be treated. If we do these things, we build with wisdom and set our lives upon the solid rock of Christ's kingdom values.

Map out your responsibilities for the day. As you do, express gratitude to God that you have all you need for today. Choose kindness and generosity in your interactions.

SUBTLE SHIFTS

"Arise, my love, my beautiful one,
and come away,
for behold, the winter is past;
the rain is over and gone."

SONG OF SOLOMON 2:10-11 ESV

For most places on earth, the seasons turn with subtlety. Spring eases into new growth, the snows melt, and the birds sing. Fall eases its way toward winter with the leaves changing color and the cooler evenings bringing an anticipation of colder days.

When we experience the subtle shifts of the seasons melting into one another, we can feel gratitude for what we've had and what will be coming as the future unfolds. Gratitude helps us see the goodness in each unique season of our lives. The cycles of life do not stop, and change is always at play. When we stop trying to resist this movement but instead learn to embrace it through mindful thankfulness, our hearts know hope, peace, and surrender in every season.

For each season, list everything you can think of that you are grateful for. Come back to this when you feel strain in the transitions.

COURAGE AND STRENGTH

On the day I called you, you answered me.
You made me strong and brave.

PSALM 138:3 NCV

When was the last time you desperately felt a need? We all are overcome with worry from time to time, but how often does relief come in an unexpected form? It is important to recognize the moments of miraculous provision in our lives so that we garner strength for today and tomorrow. God is faithful. He is a present help. He will strengthen and uphold us. He will help us through whatever comes.

Gratitude directs our attention to what is available to us. There is goodness here. There is beauty to be found now. There is provision in this place. We only have to look for it. Even as we wait, gratitude helps us find peace in the in-between. There is courage to be found in the pauses. Practicing gratitude strengthens our ability to wait patiently and with resilience.

Think through a time when an answer to a need surprised you. What good did worrying about it do? Give God your concerns—lay them all out. Then trust that he will come through as you are alert o your blessings here and now.

POWER OF PRESENCE

"I am with you always,
to the end of the age."

MATTHEW 28:20 NASB

Presence is a key to experiencing the benefits of gratitude. Gratitude helps us connect to the present moment and all the blessings that are available in it. Too often we live in the mindset of the past or future, either ruminating over what happened or trying to hedge against whatever lies ahead. When we do this, life can feel fleeting rather than engaging and enjoyable.

One of the most important results of gratitude is that it slows us down and allows us to savor moments through mindfulness. When we pay attention to where we are and who is with us, the power of engaging in the moment allows us to feel more satisfied, more connected to others, and more optimistic. Gratitude leads us back to ourselves, to our lives, and to the God who never leaves us.

Practice mindful gratitude throughout your day. When you are driving, pay attention to those around you. When you are working, tune in to the sensations of your hands at work. Engage in the moment as often as you think of it.

STAY OPEN

"Those who listen with open hearts will receive more revelation. But those who don't listen with open hearts will lose what little they think they have!"

MARK 4:25 TPT

What is the difference between an open and a closed heart? We can also think in terms of a humble person or a proud one. Maybe it makes more sense to consider life-long learners as opposed to those who are stuck in what they only know now. Curiosity is an important trait in those who are willing to listen and learn. When we think we already know everything, it is a dangerous trap of pride, and it keeps us stuck. We are all still learning, so there's no shame in admitting when we don't know something or that we got something wrong. Humility and curiosity allow openness. Listening does not mean just agreeing or disagreeing. In fact, listening with an open heart can be just that. We don't have to draw instant conclusions at all!

Gratitude can help us remain open as we look for new things to be thankful for. It opens our eyes to what we may have overlooked or taken for granted. It leans into curiosity and reveals a hunger to find the beauty around us. It only benefits us; there is no downside.

Be willing to listen with an open mind and heart when someone expresses their opinion about something.

PARTNERING WITH GOD

God is working in you, giving you the desire and the power
to do what pleases him.

PHILIPPIANS 2:13 NLT

It is encouraging to know that God works in our hearts
when we open them to him. It is empowering to know that
we can partner with his work and choose all that aligns
with his values. Gratitude helps us do this by homing in on
what truly matters. It gives us eyes to see the glorious in the
mundane. It takes away the feeling of something lacking
which we may be chasing as we learn to ground ourselves
in the goodness of where we stand.

Gratitude is a powerful builder. The more we practice it, the
more grateful we feel. In turn, the more empowered we feel
to encourage and appreciate the people in our lives. God
builds us up rather than tearing us down. He lifts us into his
life. As we choose to practice gratitude, we align with God
to build and center ourselves in that which is life-giving,
true, and beneficial to both us and others.

*Meditate on the nature of God and what impacts you
the most. As you go about your day, give thanks for these
characteristics as you choose to act in the same way.*

ACTIVE WAITING

"Remain in me, as I also remain in you. No branch can bear
fruit by itself; it must remain in the vine. Neither can you
bear fruit unless you remain in me."

JOHN 15:4 NIV

When we find ourselves waiting on God or on anything else
really, it can feel as if we are only biding our time. However,
it is in that space of waiting that we can find beautiful gifts
of grace if we are willing to look for them. Waiting is not a
waste of time; it is a necessary part of life. We can choose how
we wait. We don't have to sit on our hands or twiddle our
thumbs. We can be active in the waiting seasons of our lives.

It can be easy to connect to the bigger things in life to feel
grateful for, but what about the time we are waiting in line
at the post office or the grocery store? There are countless
opportunities for frustration in our daily lives, but there are
also just as many opportunities to flip the script and look
for good.

When you feel frustrated by something today, take a moment
to name one thing you can be grateful for in that moment.
Consider other people's perspectives, too, and offer grace
when you can.

CLINGING TO THE GOOD

Let love be without hypocrisy.
Abhor what is evil.
Cling to what is good.

ROMANS 12:9 NKJV

As we direct the inner movements of our hearts toward love and gratitude, we can show up more authentically in our relationships. We don't have to hide the times we are upset about something which needs to be addressed, but we also can be more aware of our intentions and work to manage our own narratives. Sometimes when we are upset by someone, it is because of something within us that was set off. It can end up having little to do with the other person and more to do with our own heart condition.

Clinging to the good in life does not mean that we ignore the harder aspects of it. That would be disingenuous. Loving without hypocrisy means that we don't set different standards for different people or varying circumstances. As we make choices with love as the motive, we do not turn it on or shut it off. We offer it freely, knowing love needs no reason at all to express itself. Gratitude can work the same way.

Thank God for his unmetered love that does not shift, nor does it change based on who is receiving it. Choose to love people well today.

HELP IN UNDERSTANDING

We have not received the spirit of the world, but the Spirit who comes from God, so that we may understand what has been freely given to us by God.

1 CORINTHIANS 2:12 CSB

One way to be open to receiving understanding is learning to receive help from others. Gratitude is a practice that we can do from anywhere. Still, if we feel stuck it can be helpful to know what others are thankful for. Their personal gratitude can inspire us to see things we might have overlooked in our own lives.

Just as the Holy Spirit helps us see things from God's perspective, sharing in others' gratitude can help us see our own differently. Practicing gratitude builds our thankful muscles over time, and it opens us up to recognizing reasons to be thankful in ways we would not have considered before. It can be encouraging to us and to others when we share what we are grateful for. We all need a little help in understanding, so let's not go it alone, even in our gratitude practices!

If you are feeling stuck in your gratitude practice, look up reasons that others are thankful. Seeing examples can help. Even better is sharing notes with a friend face-to-face.

GRANTED ACCESS

His divine power has granted to us all things that pertain to life and godliness, through the knowledge of him who called us to his own glory and excellence.

2 PETER 1:3 ESV

We have access to all the things that pertain to life and godliness in Christ today. There is nothing that we need that we don't have available to us today. We may think that we need more than we do because of a tendency to jump ahead to the unknown. But as we slow down and focus on today, there truly is enough. There is enough for you now no matter what your need may be.

We may have problems, but there are also solutions. We cannot control the unknowns of tomorrow, but we can choose to respond to today's challenges with creativity, gratitude, and openness. As we lean into the grace of God, we may just find the steps that leads to a solution for our immediate need.

Refuse to jump ahead of today with worry. Focus on today's responsibilities and address those with your available energy. Don't forget to make room for joy and rest, too.

SECRET OF HAPPINESS

I know how to live when I am poor, and I know how to live
when I have plenty. I have learned the secret of being happy
at any time in everything that happens, when I have enough
to eat and when I go hungry, when I have more than I need
and when I do not have enough.

PHILIPPIANS 4:12 NCV

The secret to a happy life is not in where you live. It isn't in
the purchase of all the things you wish you could buy. It's
not found in stuff at all. It is found in our attitude to life.
Our perspectives influence our satisfaction in any situation.
It is important, then, to remember that it is not what we
have that makes us content, but how we think about what
we have.

Paul said that he knew how to live in any circumstance. He
learned the secret of contentment. He found it in the grace
of God. Gratitude helps us to connect to the grace that is
present with us now. It takes intentionality and some follow
through, but the practice of gratitude truly does make us
more satisfied with our lives as they are, however they look!

*Think about your life as it stands today. Consider the
challenges, the realities, and the beauty. Spend time
connecting with the goodness that is already there.*

EMOTIONAL CONNECTION

"I will give them one heart, and put a new spirit within them. And I will remove the heart of stone from their flesh and give them a heart of flesh."

EZEKIEL 11:19 NASB

Gratitude is a powerful tool in making us feel more emotionally connected to our lives. This also includes feeling connected to our people. Instead of remaining at a distance from the people we love, gratitude draws us closer to them with love and appreciation.

Love binds us together. The practice of gratitude helps strengthen the bonds of our relationships. The two go together so well. If we want the people in our lives to know we love them, one of the best ways to do it is through gratitude. As we share our appreciation, our connections grow stronger and the love we share grows.

It is important to express our love and gratitude through words and actions. Pick at least one person in your life to intentionally share your feelings with today. Share what you love about them, how you appreciate them, and the value they bring to your life. Write them a letter or a note and sincerely express your thoughts.

WHAT CAN I DO?

"Don't worry or surrender to your fear.
For you've believed in God,
now trust and believe in me also."

JOHN 14:1 TPT

Practicing gratitude can help us when we feel the tendrils of fear and anxiety tightening around us. There can always be things we worry about, but when we choose to look for the positives, we are able to let those things go more easily. Courage isn't reserved for the fearless. It is courageous to move through the fear with faith. We don't have to feel peaceful to act with confidence. When we surrender to our fear, it sends us running or keeps us stuck. Gratitude helps us to break that cycle.

So, what can you do when you are fearful? You can direct it to the Lord. You can ground yourself in the moment you're in by acknowledging what is around you. You can focus on your breathing. You can acknowledge your feelings and know that there is more that remains true in this moment. You can practice gratitude. There are so many tools to help you work through your concerns, so don't give in to the idea that you're without hope or choices.

When you feel anxious, worried, or afraid today, choose to direct that feeling toward the Lord while also giving your attention to what you can control in this moment.

QUIET CONTEMPLATION

The LORD is good to those who depend on him,
to those who search for him.
So it is good to wait quietly
for salvation from the LORD.

LAMENTATIONS 3:25-26 NLT

Instead of focusing on the things we have, when we spend time appreciating our relationships, the importance of these people grows in our hearts. Our relationship with God counts as well. We may find a bit of joy in material possessions, but we are created for connection with others, and we'll experience deeper joy in those relationships than we ever could with our stuff.

Contemplation is a beautiful tool to help us be aware and to turn our focus intentionally. We can use quiet contemplation as part of our gratitude practice. As we contemplate the important relationships in our lives, let's not forget to turn our hearts toward God. He is near, and his goodness is already present with us.

Take some time to think about the people you love today.
What do you appreciate about them?

ROOM FOR BOTH

Immediately the boy's father exclaimed,
"I do believe; help me overcome my unbelief!"

MARK 9:24 NIV

Gratitude doesn't remove us from reality, and it doesn't make us delusional. It connects us to points of goodness that are as real as the ground we walk upon. Gratitude is not theoretical; it is rooted in God's purpose for us, his creation. Still, it is important to realize it is not a solution to our problems. It will not make them go away. It will, however, change our perspectives and may affect how we approach different issues.

There is room for both our beliefs as well as our struggles to believe. God sees our hearts, and he is faithful to his Word no matter what we're going through. Our own hearts can grow in trust as we practice gratitude regularly. As our eyes are tuned to the goodness that we already are living with, our ability to hope for more strengthens. Our satisfaction with what already is real grows. If we are struggling to believe, let's remember what he has said is true and how he has already come through for his people.

If you have experienced an answer to prayer, take time to meditate on the experience. As it comes to mind, give thanks all over again. Let your gratitude lead you in prayer.

SEPTEMBER

Let us come into his presence
with thanksgiving;
let us make a joyful noise to him
with songs of praise!

PSALM 95:2 ESV

SETTLED

May the God of all grace, who called us to His eternal glory by Christ Jesus, after you have suffered a while, perfect, establish, strengthen, and settle you.

1 PETER 5:10 NKJV

Suffering is an unavoidable part of life. We lose loved ones, we deal with health issues, and there are other hardships. We cannot avoid pain, but we can find relief in it. Gratitude has been linked to lower pain levels, higher optimism, and greater resilience in those who practice it. Gratitude helps us look outside ourselves to the beauty in the world and in the people around us. We feel more settled as we incorporate gratitude into our lives.

Gratitude does not help us escape reality. It engages us with our feelings of peacefulness. We can be going through a hard time and still find reasons to be thankful. More than just naming what we are thankful for, we can pause and allow the emotions to fill us. As we do, it impacts our well-being in far broader ways than just our cognition.

Pause for a moment after you consider each thing you are grateful for today. Name it, think about it, and stay there until you feel gratitude expanding your heart and allowing peace to descend.

MADE FOR THIS TIME

He has made everything appropriate in its time. He has also put eternity in their hearts, but no one can discover the work God has done from beginning to end.

ECCLESIASTES 3:11 CSB

The New Living Translation begins today's verse this way: "God has made everything beautiful for its own time." We are not accidents walking around as we try to make our way through life. God created us with inherent beauty, purpose, and creativity. Where we are in the history of the world is not by chance. It may have taken a lot of variables to get us here, but we are in our time and place for a reason.

Have you ever wished to live during a different era? Though this is a natural thought, the truth is that you can find your intention and satisfaction here in this moment that you are living. You weren't set upon the earth at another time; this is your time. It is easy to focus on the negative things happening around us in the world, but that won't help us to grow in quietude or contentment. Incorporating gratitude helps us see the gifts we have at our fingertips. It aids us in engaging with the lives we are living, not the ones we wished we had.

Look closely at your life. Where you live, the people around you, and your capabilities are specifically designed for you. Give thanks for the ones that stand out the most today.

WITH CONFIDENCE

Let us then with confidence draw near to the throne of grace, that we may receive mercy and find grace to help in time of need.

HEBREWS 4:16 ESV

Awareness moves us to gratitude, which in turn leads us to confidence. When we become aware of everything in our day to be thankful for, we willingly offer heartfelt gratitude for it. The more we practice gratitude, the more we discover all the wonder and beauty there is to be grateful for even in the mess of things.

There are some people who welcome you with open arms no matter how or when you come to them. Who is the friend you call when you're in trouble? Who do you welcome into your home when it is messy, and you haven't showered yet? These relationships are built on trust and have a closeness that allows for confidence. In your relationship with Christ, the more time you spend with him, the more you realize that he welcomes you however you are and whenever you come to him. He's always available and more than ready to help.

Reach out to someone who is there for you whenever you need them. Buy them something small that shows you care about them such as coffee or a book.

NEVER WITHOUT HELP

He gives strength to those who are tired
and more power to those who are weak.

ISAIAH 40:29 NCV

One of the most powerful affirmations we have is being
seen. When someone notices us by asking how we are
doing, sending a note, or acknowledging something that
we did, it can be very validating. Perfection has nothing
to do with life satisfaction. It evades us all. But being seen,
known, and cared for is incredibly valuable.

If we are not careful, we can let moments of being seen pass
by without acknowledging them. Gratitude helps us home
in on these times and savor them as they are happening. We
can engage with others as well by offering our appreciation.
As we do, we will easily realize that connection with others
is a very important part of our lives indeed.

*Take time to connect with people in various ways. Smile at a
stranger, have a conversation with a coworker, and go out to
dinner with friends. However, you can engage and interact
with others in gratitude, do it.*

TAKE THE TIME

"Come away by yourselves to a secluded place and rest a little while." (For there were many people coming and going, and they did not even have time to eat.)

MARK 6:31 NASB

Take time to nourish your soul as well as your body. It is important that we incorporate rhythms of rest into our schedules. If we don't, we will become burned out and without the reserves to offer much of ourselves to those closest to us. Some people call this rest space the margin. It is the blank area we preserve in our lives which acts as a natural buffer.

Getting our nourishment takes intention and time. Our gratitude practices can help us zero in on what matters most. As we mark these qualities that are so important to us, we can discern what we need to make more room for in our lives. Perhaps the planning makes the effort of turning down other opportunities a bit clearer. We can only protect that which we are aware of. Gratitude can help us set our priorities straight, build better boundaries, and allow for joyfulness in our offerings of service.

Take time to schedule restful activities this week. Put it on your calendar. Make appointments for yourself to read a book, meet up with a friend, or lay in bed. Whatever feels restful to you can help nourish your soul.

MERCY IN ACTION

Jesus ministered from place to place throughout all of the province of Galilee. He taught in the synagogues, preaching the wonderful news of the kingdom and healing every kind of sickness and disease among the people.

MATTHEW 4:23 TPT

The more grateful we are, the more willing we are to be gracious with others. This isn't just a nice thought; it's backed up by research and various studies. The studies show that those who practice gratitude—with more than a periodic thank-you—tend to give others more benefit of the doubt, are more likely to be engaged with their communities, and are more generous with their resources.

It stands to reason, then, that if we want to be more merciful and live the way Jesus did, gratitude is an important aspect of building our lifestyles of love. We can choose love at any point, but gratitude makes us choose it more readily. When we realize how much there is to be thankful for, we are motivated to share it with others.

Reflect on patterns of your gratitude. What about your practice has come up time and again? What stands out? How can you choose love and share it with someone today?

ENOUGH TO GO AROUND

This same God who takes care of me will supply all your needs from his glorious riches, which have been given to us in Christ Jesus.

PHILIPPIANS 4:19 NLT

There are limited resources in this world, but God's resources are endless. There is always enough love, kindness, restoration, peace, and joy to go around. When we practice gratitude, we begin to see the abundance of what is available to us from God. As we engage with thankfulness for these things, we are much more generous with what we have. And we are hopeful for what lies ahead.

Gratitude can inspire us to make plans for the coming days by empowering us to see the fruit of yesterday's efforts. All in all, gratitude aligns our perspectives with God's abundance and the reality of his mercy in our lives. There is enough to go around, so there's no need to entertain a fear-based hoarding habit for whatever we have.

Do something kind for someone today with a generous heart.

SAME PURPOSE

The plans of the LORD stand firm forever,
the purposes of his heart through all generations.

PSALM 33:11 NIV

The purpose of the Lord never changes. His character is steadfast throughout every age and each generation. He is always full of loyal love, abounding peace, and powerful salvation. Though our understanding of him may change, he never does. When we make gratitude a part of our lives, we prioritize the important things in life. It may help us clarify what our own purpose is, and it need not be anything fancier than to love well.

Though the Lord is unchanging, he is always doing something new. The same can be true for our practices of gratitude. The purpose remains the same—to connect to what is good, what we appreciate in others, and the beauty around us—but the way we go about it may change. A fresh approach may be all we need to experience deeper gratitude in our lives.

If you can, spend time doing something that brings you joy. If you're not able to, imagine yourself doing it and thank the Lord for the delight you find in it.

ALWAYS ABOUNDING

Be steadfast, immovable, always abounding in the work of the Lord, knowing that your labor is not in vain in the Lord.

1 CORINTHIANS 15:58 NKJV

Gratitude is a wonderful motivator. Shame is a terrible one. Rather than trying to coerce ourselves or others into doing what needs to be done, let's take time to do it from a place of gratitude. Does the lawn need mowing? Instead of dreading it, can you thank God for the land you inhabit or for the benefit you receive from being outside?

The work that needs to be done may not cease, but our attitudes about it can be realigned. The mundane can feel overwhelming, but it is in these precise places where we can experience deep satisfaction as we incorporate thankful hearts. There is grace that allows us to see things from a different, more hopeful perspective today.

Instead of avoiding tasks that you dread, take a minute to see some of the benefits of doing them. Once you do, give thanks, and then re-engage in them.

SIMPLE AND TRUE

We love because he first loved us.

1 JOHN 4:19 CSB

We learn to love well from the source of love himself. As we fill up with his love, it overflows into our own relationships. When we look at the time Jesus Christ spent on earth, what we see is a life poured out in mercy. He has so much grace, kindness, and peace to offer those who look to him. May we be like him. May we love without borders or excuses.

Gratitude directly links to our expressions of love. What we feel thankful for, we will share with others, and that includes how we treat them. Let's give our appreciation and encouragement like it's going out of style. Let's endeavor to love better than we ever have before. If we are going to strive for anything, let's work to love everyone in our lives well.

Consider the most recent way you felt loved by someone. Return the favor or pay it forward today.

ENCOURAGING WISDOM

Let the word of Christ dwell in you richly, teaching and admonishing one another in all wisdom, singing Psalms and hymns and spiritual songs, with thankfulness in your hearts to God.

COLOSSIANS 3:16 ESV

Wisdom is instructive and life-giving. Even when it causes us to correct our course of action, it doesn't induce us to shame. It is full of encouragement and truth. God is full of wisdom and full of love. Love is a wonderful motivator; it builds us up instead of breaking us down. Wisdom doesn't shy away from the truth, but it also doesn't depart from love.

Pride can disguise itself as wisdom. Gratitude helps us remain humble and open while also maintaining truth as our foundation. As we practice thankfulness, we train our minds to look for the good that is at work in our daily lives. It is not fantasy; it is integrated with reality. Wisdom is also grounded in truth while it calls us to see things from a different perspective. When we are willing to approach things differently, we remain open to wisdom's voice.

Gratitude is a powerful practice that helps us see the positives which balance the negative aspects of our lives. When you give advice or offer constructive criticism today, make sure you are encouraging in your tone and your intentions.

SURROUNDED BY GRACE

He found them in a desert,
a windy, empty land.
He surrounded them and brought them up,
guarding them as those he loved very much.

DEUTERONOMY 32:10 NCV

There is grace around us if we have eyes to see it. It comes from many simple, unexpected sources such as comfort offered by friends, support of your community, safety in a home with four strong walls, food in the kitchen, and a warm bed to sleep in. When we turn our eyes to the basic needs of our beings, we can uncover that which we may take for granted. If we look for bigger, better things that make our lives look less impressive, we miss out on enjoying what blessings are already ours.

Comparison can quickly lead to envy and covetousness. But the practice of gratitude directs our focus back to what is already ours. As we consciously give thanks for the good things in our lives, we naturally feel deep satisfaction. Even on hard days when all we are grateful for is being alive, it is still a good reason to be thankful, nonetheless.

Take some time to think through all the basic needs you have that are already met. Give thanks for each one, taking time to focus on the significance of the basics and their blessings.

A SENSE OF BELONGING

"Do not fear, for I have redeemed you;
I have called you by name; you are Mine!"

ISAIAH 43:1 NASB

Gratitude can help us feel less isolated from the people in our lives. Often what brings us deep fulfillment is our relationships. We were created for community and connection. As we focus on reasons to be grateful, the people in our lives will account for a large portion of those reasons.

Mutuality in our relationships allows us to feel seen, understood, and empowered to offer the same gift to others. One-sided relationships don't often stand the test of time. They are imbalanced. Christ chose us in love, and we offer him our love in response. Gratitude for the people in our lives helps us strengthen the bonds we now have and makes those bonds stronger. We are then more motivated to offer unreserved acknowledgment and encouragement to our friends, family, and coworkers.

Look at your closest relationships with fresh eyes today. Consider at least three things that you are grateful for in the person you are thinking about. Share an encouragement or a note of appreciation with them.

THOUGHTS IN THE NIGHT

In the middle of the night I awake to give thanks to you
because of all your revelation-light—so right and true!

PSALM 119:62 TPT

What kinds of thoughts wake you up in the middle of
the night? For some of us, the early hours can be a time
when we are bombarded with worries or our minds whirl
in anticipation of stressful situations. Lying awake and
ruminating on these things can feel overwhelming and just
plain frustrating.

The practice of gratitude has been shown to improve sleep
patterns in those who practice it before going to bed.
Right before sleep is a great time to write a couple things
in our gratitude journals, recalling what we are grateful
for in the day that has passed. Apart from this, we can also
use prayer when we wake up in the middle of the night,
turning our hearts to God and offering him all that we are
worried about. This makes it easier to focus on the things
we are thankful for. Perhaps instead of counting sheep, we
can count our blessings until we fall back into a peaceful
slumber.

Before you go to sleep tonight, write down all that you are
grateful for in your day. If you wake up, continue to count
your blessings until you feel peace begin to fill your mind and
your heart.

EVERY CIRCUMSTANCE

Love never gives up, never loses faith, is always hopeful,
and endures through every circumstance.

1 CORINTHIANS 13:7 NLT

Love never gives up. Every circumstance is improved
when love is the enduring motivator. For as long as there
is love, there is hope. There is belonging. There is peace.
Love endures through whatever we experience. This is
exceedingly good news.

When we focus on the lasting things such as the goodness
that is true and present in our lives no matter what the
season, we can offer gratitude. We can connect with
thankfulness anywhere and in any circumstance. Studies
show that those who practice gratitude have higher
resilience and more patience. Such a simple but powerful
tool helps us endure even the hardest times with grace,
hope, and love.

*Write down every expression of love that is present in your
life now. When you are finished with your list, read it over
carefully. By being intentional and specific, you draw your
attention to the reality of the love that never gives up, never
loses faith, and never leaves. Love is present in so many forms!*

JOYOUS WISDOM

How happy your people must be! How happy your officials,
who continually stand before you and hear your wisdom!

2 CHRONICLES 9:7 NIV

One of the most powerful and effective ways to cultivate
joy in our lives is to practice gratitude. Intentionally
incorporating thankfulness as a daily exercise means that
we reap the benefits of strengthening this muscle and
growing it over time. Joyful satisfaction with our lives will
not happen by accident, at least not in a resilient, enduring
way. Joy need not be dependent on our circumstances at all.
It is all about how we look at those circumstances.

We embrace growth in our daily lives as we practice
gratitude. We must be willing to look through our lenses a
bit differently if we want to experience more joy. We don't
have to wait to experience joy in order to be grateful. The
practice of gratitude can make us feel more joy in the lives
we are already living!

*You don't have to feel exuberant about the things you're
grateful for in order to truly appreciate them. Joy will come.
Take turns sharing one thing you are grateful for with people
you love during a meal or over coffee.*

WORDS MATTER

Death and life are in the power of the tongue,
And those who love it will eat its fruit.

PROVERBS 18:21 NKJV

We can build others up or tear them down with our words.
We should not be careless with anything we say to one
another. When we approach others with kindness, respect,
and humility, we will be strengthened by it.

Gratitude helps us treat others better because it allows us
to see the good in them before we say a word. When we
practice gratitude in our relationships, we can build and
strengthen our bonds by expressing what we are thankful
for. We may not think much about a careless word that we
toss out, but that does not mean it is harmless. At every
point we decide how we approach others, so let's take
ownership of how we do that today. As we incorporate
gratitude into our lives, we become more gracious and
encouraging people.

In your interactions with others, choose words that offer life,
love, and encouragement even when giving some necessary
feedback. As far as you are able, build others up.

COMBATING MATERIALISM

The one who loves silver is never satisfied with silver,
and whoever loves wealth is never satisfied with income.
This too is futile.

ECCLESIASTES 5:10 CSB

Research supports what today's verse says. Those who are
materialistic seem to have a hard time feeling satisfied since
they are always searching for more. Because they can never
attain that goal, no matter how much they have, satisfaction
eludes them. The good news is that no matter how we have
approached this in the past, we can combat materialism by
regularly practicing gratitude starting now.

As we learn to find appreciation for what we now own, our
contentment grows. Studies show that grateful people give
more money to charity. This is remarkable. It doesn't matter
how much we have but rather how we perceive what we
have that influences our generosity! If we want to be more
generous with our resources, one of the best places to boost
this impulse is with our gratitude practices. What a simple
way to grow in God's heart and to be more like him.

*As an act of gratitude, choose to share a resource you have
with someone else today.*

JUST ENOUGH

We brought nothing into the world, and we cannot take anything out of the world. But if we have food and clothing, with these we will be content.

1 TIMOTHY 6:7-8 ESV

We don't need an abundance of belongings to be grateful for what we have. We can be thankful for "just enough" which covers our basic needs. If we approach today as it is and look for reasons to be grateful, we will find them. We can't control the day we're born or the day we leave this earth, or a myriad of other things in between. We can, however, choose how we approach what we have each moment.

If we turn our attention to what is already enough, we may be astounded by what we find. Let's not overlook this part of our gratitude practice, for it can bring peace, focus, and even motivation as we look toward the future.

What do you have enough of today? Perhaps you feel a need. Write your needs for today first, then make a column for what you have that is already enough for today. Perhaps writing the latter made your needs feel less. If it did, thank God for the power of this practice and trust him with the rest.

RICHES OF KNOWLEDGE

I thank God because in Christ you have been made rich in every way, in all your speaking and in all your knowledge.

1 CORINTHIANS 1:5 NCV

Gratitude creates an inner richness as we practice it. It doesn't cost a thing, yet it builds an internal world that is wealthy in appreciation, love, and grace. There is more than enough hope to be found in the lives we are already living. There is an abundance of joy in the present moment. There is peace in the gifts of goodness which we can now experience.

Gratitude is not tied to our circumstances, and it doesn't need to be connected to any specific event. As we meditate on the valuable things in our lives, we realize that we already have treasures in our midst. There is always something worth appreciating in this present moment. When we look for these treasures, we train our minds to do this more and more. As we create spaces to hold our appreciation, we collect riches to both cherish and to share with others.

Go out of your way to share your gratitude with someone.

INEXPRESSIBLE JOY

Though you have not seen Him, you love Him, and though you do not see Him now, but believe in Him, you greatly rejoice with joy inexpressible and full of glory.

1 PETER 1:8 NASB

It is true that we can love what is outside of what we can see. Though we do not see Christ with our physical eyes, we know his presence in our hearts and in the evidence of our lives. He has given us his goodness. We may not look at him the way we look at those with whom we interact daily, but that does not mean that his Spirit is not with us.

Gratitude helps us see from a different perspective. It gives us eyes to see the evidence of God's goodness which is present with us. We rejoice in the beauty that is so accessible. As we do this on a regular basis, our joy increases. It has been found that some of the most genuinely joyful people are the most grateful ones. What an important connection this is to remember!

Give someone in your life a genuine compliment based on something you appreciate about them. Be sure to use a specific example that illustrates your appreciation.

AMAZING HOPE

With this amazing hope living in us, we step out in freedom
and boldness to speak the truth.

2 CORINTHIANS 3:12 TPT

Gratitude is linked to a higher sense of self as well as a
feeling of confidence in those who practice it regularly.
When we choose to look for the good in others, we also
may begin to see and appreciate our own inherent value.
With a greater sense of confidence comes a freedom in
living authentically and generously.

Truth requires boldness. Fear can keep us from saying the
hard things that people may disagree with, but it does not
mean that we must give in to that fear. When we know what
is truly important and the things worth bringing to light,
we can move in boldness and freedom to speak the truth
in love. Gratitude connects us to the truth of what is good,
and it also directs us to the amazing hope we have in life
with Christ. What an amazing tool this is to live with the
values of God's kingdom in full view.

*When you are bothered by something that someone says
or does today, consider whether it is a value issue or an
annoyance. Speak the truth in love and extend grace even as
you encourage them to see from a different perspective.*

DEEPLY ROOTED

Let your roots grow down into him, and let your lives be built on him. Then your faith will grow strong in the truth you were taught, and you will overflow with thankfulness.

COLOSSIANS 2:7 NLT

When we build our lives on the foundation of Christ and his kingdom, we align ourselves with his values. Gratitude is a powerful path to focusing on what matters to him and consequently to us as well. If we are starting to grow in understanding, there might even be some overlap.

The grace of gratitude helps us remain open to different ways of looking at the world, to the kindness that is present today, and to the gifts of goodness that reveal the mercy of God's heart. The more we practice gratitude, the more rooted we become in the reality of God's goodness. The more rooted we become, the more delight we experience in our lives. The more delight we experience, the more we are motivated to help others. There are so many benefits!

We don't have to wait to give thanks though the more we practice gratitude, the more easily it will flow. Read through a gratitude list that you made on another day and see if that sparks any more thankfulness in your heart.

NOT A SLAVE

You are no longer a slave, but God's child;
and since you are his child,
God has made you also an heir.

GALATIANS 4:7 NIV

As children of God, we are heirs to his promise. Our hope is not in vain, for we have a faithful Father who follows through on his Word. We are found in him, so we are not slaves to our impulses. We are free in his mercy.

The practice of gratitude frees us from the bondage we may fear. Instead of getting lost in the what ifs, we can ground ourselves in the truth of what really is. There is goodness here. There are pockets of peace. There is beauty. There is life, and that life is a gift. Whenever we feel bound, and whatever cycles we may feel stuck in, gratitude can be a powerful tool to break us out of it. It alerts us to the realities of goodness and to the possibilities in front of us.

Take some time when you are in a calm state of mind to take note of the things that you are grateful for. When you feel yourself being pulled into old patterns, take out your list and read it. Read it aloud if you can and remind yourself that there is goodness here.

LOST AND FOUND

"The Son of Man has come to seek and to save
that which was lost."

LUKE 19:10 NKJV

Have you ever wondered where the passion you once held
for your life went? Perhaps you used to feel an ease that
is now inaccessible. Joy is not reserved for the calm times
in life. You can learn to access it through the power and
practice of gratitude.

Just as Christ came to seek and save that which was lost, we
can find more than we thought possible in our lives just as
they are now. What was lost before, is now found in him.
We change as we grow, but that does not mean happier days
are behind us. We can find satisfaction and contentment as
we engage with the goodness already hidden in our daily
lives. There is beauty, there is connection, and there is life.
There is more than you can possibly know, but the joy is in
uncovering what is already there with the eyes of someone
on a true treasure hunt.

*Spend time praying before your gratitude practice today. Ask
the Spirit to open your eyes to the treasures of goodness and
the joy in your life that is hiding in plain sight.*

INNER SATISFACTION

"Whoever drinks from the water that I will give him will never get thirsty again. In fact, the water I will give him will become a well of water springing up in him for eternal life."

JOHN 4:14 CSB

Deep wells of gladness reside in our inner beings. For most of us to access them, we must do some digging. Gratitude helps us dig deeper, and as we continue to practice, we make headway in uncovering the satisfaction of a life fed by the living waters of God's goodness.

We receive the gift of eternal life as we join our hearts and lives with Christ. The wells of life which spring from his presence can be continually accessed to refresh our souls. Gratitude is one way to connect to his presence in tangible ways. It trains our minds to look for wherever he is already working on us. He is not far off. He's not at a distance. He is near, and gratitude helps us have the vision to see more clearly where he is.

Go outside and pick up something in nature. Hold it and say what you are grateful for in this moment. Connect to your gratitude in a physical way.

HEALING RAYS

"For you who fear my name, the sun of righteousness
shall rise with healing in its wings."

MALACHI 4:2 ESV

Gratitude is like a flower opening to the sun. It points us
to where the light shines. We turn toward it and soak in its
rays. In the light of truth, we find peace, love, hope, and
joy. We find refreshment and rest. As we open our hearts in
gratitude, we swing wide the doors of our hearts and let the
Son shine on us.

The effects of gratitude on our well-being are supported by
science, but its benefits started long before we knew these
things. We honor God by choosing gratitude, but gratitude
benefits us more than we can ever imagine. Isn't this so like
God? He knows what is good for us and what will bring
us life in all its forms. Why not trust him and do as he has
encouraged us to do?

*Consider an area of your life where you have been
procrastinating. Start taking steps toward whatever it is that
you know you should be doing. Ask God for wisdom, thank
him for his help, and pinpoint one thing you can do this
week—today if you can—that will start the process.*

HE ALREADY KNOWS

"Don't be like them, because your Father knows the things you need before you ask him."

MATTHEW 6:8 NCV

Jesus encouraged his followers to be simple in their prayers and with their words. There is no magic formula to getting God to listen to us. We don't have to use specific words or try to sound holy. God already knows our needs, and we don't have to beg him to pay attention to us. A simple heartfelt prayer is better than a fancy one that aspires to be heard by others.

Gratitude helps us simplify our expectations and our lives by giving us eyes to see the goodness in ordinary things. We don't need more to be happier. In fact, that is counterintuitive, and it doesn't work that way. Gratitude cultivates a heart that recognizes there is power in the simplest forms.

Use the Lord's prayer in your gratitude practice today. You can find it in Matthew 6:9-13. As you pray it, thank God that you don't need to reach for anything else. He sees, he knows, and he hears. So, he will answer.

OUTSIDE OURSELVES

Know that the LORD Himself is God;
It is He who has made us, and not we ourselves;
We are His people and the sheep of His pasture.

PSALM 100:3 NASB

Our origin stories never truly start with us. We were created thoughtfully and uniquely in the heart of God. We are his handiwork. We are expressions of his creativity. Starting with that knowledge, let's be grateful for our personalities, our quirks, and the different ways we live and move.

We are one small part of a larger whole. Gratitude helps us see outside ourselves even as we give thanks for who we are. The kinder we are to ourselves, the kinder we will be to others. Gratitude leads to compassion which leads to generosity. We don't have to know what someone else is going through in order to offer them grace; we can give it regardless. Though it starts in our hearts, it affects everyone we interact with.

Find five things you love or are thankful for in or around yourself. When you interact with others, look for the good in them as well.

REFLECTIONS OF MERCY

His unforgettable works of surpassing wonder
reveal his grace and tender mercy.

PSALM 111:4 TPT

The miracles of God are reflections of his mercy. The power of his saving grace, his refuge in times of trouble, and his resurrection life, are all revelations of his tender love. Love shouts from the rooftops and it whispers in the dark. It is not simply one thing. It is reflected in the way someone supports another as well as in the humble act of covering expenses without the recipient knowing. The power of God is present in both big choices and little actions. Can we not express gratitude in the same way?

Our practices of gratitude needn't look the same every day. We can be loud about it one day and quiet on another. Thankfulness is as true when we're holding something precious in our hearts as when we're showing up for the people we love. Let's not diminish true gratefulness down to one expression for it is a perspective and a lifestyle. Its expressions can be as varied as love in all its forms!

Take some time to tune in to your emotions today. Are you tender or hopeful? Fired up or thoughtful? Express your gratitude in line with how you are feeling as a true expression of where you're at today.

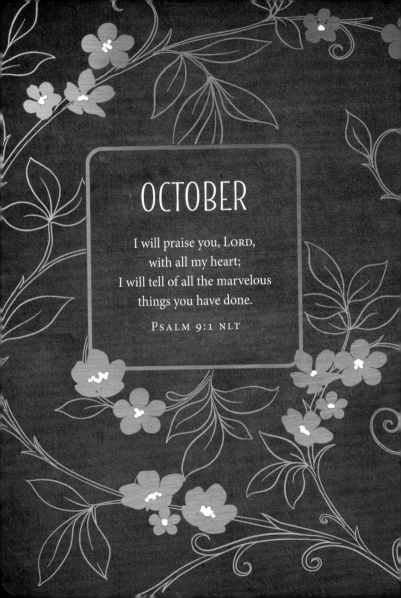

OCTOBER

I will praise you, LORD,
with all my heart;
I will tell of all the marvelous
things you have done.

PSALM 9:1 NLT

POSSIBILITIES OF BREAKTHROUGH

"All this may seem impossible to you now, a small remnant of God's people. But is it impossible for me?"

ZECHARIAH 8:6 NLT

When we're lost in the what ifs of tomorrow or the regrets of yesterday, we may find it hard to hold on to hope. As we learn to be grounded in the present through gratitude, we find that there are reasons to hope, giving even the simplest forms of relief. We don't have to have all the details about the future in order to trust that it will be okay. We just need to feel secure in hope.

When it is especially hard to find things to be thankful for, it may help to remember the way God provided in the past. We are here today with breath in our lungs and opportunities in each day, even if the opportunity today is simply to be where we are. We can draw courage by remembering the hard times we have gone through and reframing our current challenges through the lens of opportunity.

Look through your camera roll over the past year. Allow yourself to connect with every good moment that each picture suggests.

MOTIVATION OF EXPECTATION

Jesus got up and went with him, and so did his disciples. Just then a woman who had been subject to bleeding for twelve years came up behind him and touched the edge of his cloak.

MATTHEW 9:19-20 NIV

Our expectations drive our actions. If we don't expect a favorable response from someone, we are less likely to take the risk to reach out to them. If we anticipate rejection, we won't reach for new opportunities. Gratitude connects us with the goodness in our lives, which leads to greater confidence. The more confidence we have, the more our expectations will shift.

This is not a trick; it is a powerful tool. Our outlook influences the actions we are willing to take. Wherever we focus our attentions, our behaviors soon follow. Practicing gratitude allows us to be more gracious and grateful people. It drives us to take chances that we might have talked ourselves out of. The woman in today's verse was desperate, but she also knew who Jesus was. Her expectation of healing drove her to get as close to Jesus as she could, and we know how that turned out. Gratitude will shape our expectations, so let's remember to keep it a priority.

The next time you feel vulnerable when taking a risk, consider what the biggest gains could be. Ground yourself in gratitude and proceed.

LEARNED BEHAVIOR

Not that I speak in regard to need, for I have learned in whatever state I am, to be content.

PHILIPPIANS 4:11 NKJV

The principle of practice is important with gratitude. The more we do something, the more natural it becomes. It doesn't matter if we have lived with pessimism, or we struggle to see the bright side of things. The practice of gratitude is shown to make those who use it more optimistic over time. If you want a more positive outlook, you can learn it!

In the same way, if you want to have more contentment in your life, the way to cultivate it is not in some far-off goal. If our level of contentment is based on achieving those feelings someday, it is not true contentment at all. True contentment is found in the lives we have now. And we can learn to be gratified in our lives by incorporating thankfulness.

Decide how you want to incorporate gratitude into your days over the next week. Do you want to keep writing in a gratitude journal? Do you want to share your thankfulness with a friend over texts each day? Commit to following through on it regardless of which method you choose.

HUMBLE YOURSELF

Instruct those who are rich in the present age not to be arrogant or to set their hope on the uncertainty of wealth, but on God, who richly provides us with all things to enjoy.

1 TIMOTHY 6:17 CSB

Pride leads us into thinking too highly of ourselves. Most of us can spot a haughty attitude in ourselves, but how many of us are willing to overlook it in our perfectionistic tendencies? Perfectionism is an unrealistic standard. It requires that in order to be good, we must do everything right, and get it right the first time. This, my friend, is a form of pride. It puts too much emphasis on what we can do and not enough on the grace that God offers us.

What if you saw your imperfections as an opportunity, rather than a reason to be ashamed? Each time you don't meet your own expectations, thank God that his ways are better than yours. Thank him for not expecting perfection from you. Thank him that he's with you in your mistakes. Thank him for the grace that he gives to keep moving forward.

When you spot perfectionism in your expectations, take a moment to audibly thank God that you are not what you do. Choose to let go of the need to show up perfectly.

SUPPORTIVE COMMUNITY

The full number of those who believed were of one heart and soul, and no one said that any of the things that belonged to him was his own, but they had everything in common.

ACTS 4:32 ESV

Gratitude connects us to the people in our lives with compassion and humility. It helps us offer grace and space to each other. The more gracious we are, the more generously we behave. This is what research shows, and it is easy to see that this is the way that God designed us all along.

If we want to be more supportive of people, a wonderful way to do that is to keep practicing gratitude. As we do this, we end up looking for the goodness in others. As we become attuned to where others are at, we are also more aware of the needs they may have. Gratitude for what we have can motivate us to share with others. It is a connective practice, not just a personal one.

Pay attention to the people around you today. If you see a need that you can meet, reach out and offer to do it.

PERFECT EXAMPLE

This is what you were called to do, because Christ suffered
for you and gave you an example to follow.
So you should do as he did.

1 PETER 2:21 NCV

There are many examples of people doing good in the
world. There are everyday heroes among us who generously
share what they have in order to help others in many ways.
Let's not give in to the notion that the world is awful and
there are no good people. There are always people doing
impactful work; we only need to look for them.

Christ is our greatest example. When we live with his values
guiding our actions, we become more like him. The truth
is that there are many people being the light of Christ in
the world, doing the work that most people do not want
to. They lead with love, unconcerned about power and
prestige, and they follow Jesus' ways.

*Give thanks for the good people you know, the people who
have made a difference in your life and in their communities.
Reach out to them and encourage them today.*

BANNER OF LOVE

"He has brought me to his banquet hall,
And his banner over me is love."

SONG OF SOLOMON 2:4 NASB

Gratitude helps us to see the love of God playing out in our lives. It gives us vision for that mercy that meets us in the details. Our lives are not without the presence of God and the fullness of his nature. We are covered by his great love for us, for his banner over us is love.

When we know how thoroughly, how wonderfully loved we are, we cannot help but be changed by the knowledge. Our confidence grows, we become more generous and empathetic, and we love others as they should be. There is room to be human in God's love, which means there's room for all of us, including all our mistakes and our misunderstandings. We are welcomed to the table as whole people, and God delights in us. This is bound to transform us! Gratitude reminds us that we are seated at the banquet table of God, and it is his invitation that brought us to him in the first place.

When you feel as if you are not enough today, remember with thankfulness that you have been offered a seat at God's table, and he knows exactly who you are!

PROVISION ALL AROUND

"Consider the birds—do you think they worry about their existence? They don't plant or reap or store up food, yet your heavenly Father provides them each with food. Aren't you much more valuable to your Father than they?"

MATTHEW 6:26 TPT

Some days feel harder than others, even if nothing on the outside seems to have changed. Don't use hard days to heap shame on yourself. You might be tempted to tell yourself that you should feel better, but that won't help anything. Instead of distancing yourself from your feelings, try accepting them as they are without judgment. This is a mindfulness practice that can help you become more compassionate with yourself. Even if you do not know the reason for your emotional state, you can still be gentle on yourself, just as God is gentle with you.

Gratitude shifts our focus from the hard challenges to the good blessings. It is not an emotion-bypassing activity, but a perspective-shifting one. When we give thanks for what is true, beautiful, and sufficient today, it can help us feel better about the things that aren't.

When you feel overwhelmed today, put your hand over your heart, remind yourself where you are physically, and remember that you are so loved. You are taken care of. You are seen.

LOOSENING OUR GRIP

"If you try to hang on to your life, you will lose it.
But if you give up your life for my sake, you will save it."

MATTHEW 16:25 NLT

The more tightly we hold on to things, the harder it can be to embrace change when it becomes necessary in our spiritual growth. We are not promised an easy life. Everyone faces challenges and hardships. There is not one person alive who is exempt from trials and tribulations! However, we can grow in resiliency as we practice gratitude. Throughout the shifts and changes of this life, we can more easily roll with the punches when we actively seek goodness in our lives.

Gratitude may help us more easily let go of the things we can't change and turn with thankfulness to what is still true. There may be pain, but there is also joy. There is also hope and opportunity. Grieving what has been lost is necessary, but so is gratitude for what remains and what is to come. As we remember this, we root ourselves in the present and give our hearts reasons to hope for tomorrow.

When you feel yourself resisting change, try reframing the narrative. Give thanks for what it was and recognize that there is goodness and opportunity in letting go.

WONDERS TO BEHOLD

"Listen to this, Job;
stop and consider God's wonders."

JOB 37:14 NIV

When we are caught up in the busyness of our lives, it takes intentionality to zoom out for a broader perspective. We find gratitude in our own details, but we also find it outside of ourselves. When we take time to consider God's wonders, we connect to the goodness of his power at work in the world.

Gratitude is as much a perspective and heart posture as it is a character trait. We can develop gratitude in many ways; the important thing is that we do it. For some of us, learning about the intricacies of nature opens new levels of gratitude. For others, the mysteries of space make us marvel at the majesty of God. Whatever draws us into wonder is a good thing. Let's make the time and space to move toward awe today.

Engage in an activity that engages your wonder in the world. It could even just mean watching a documentary, reading a scientific article, or going out to star-gaze. Simply move toward awe and give thanks for the ability to experience it today.

NURTURING COMFORT

"As one whom his mother comforts,
So I will comfort you;
And you shall be comforted in Jerusalem."

ISAIAH 66:13 NKJV

There is nothing like the comforting arms of our loving caregivers. They soothed our wounds and our sadness when we were younger. They offered us protection, care, and comfort when we needed it. We will never outgrow the longing for nurture in times of distress. In God, we have an attentive and caring Father. He draws us in with love and comforts us.

Gratitude can compel us to be compassionate toward others. We are more caring as we become attuned to the people around us. The power of gratitude does not begin or end with us. It always leads to being more generous and gracious toward others. It is an inherently connective activity. The more grateful we are for the people in our lives, the more we are willing to show it. The more we show it, the stronger our relationships become.

If you see someone struggling today, offer comfort and compassion in a practical way.

ALERT AND AWARE

"Be alert, because you don't know
either the day or the hour."

MATTHEW 25:13 CSB

One way to become more alert in our lives is to practice
gratitude. Instead of letting time simply pass us by, we
engage it by acknowledging and cherishing the things we
are grateful for each day. It is a practice that connects us
to the moment, and in turn we become more aware of the
goodness within our lives and in the world around us.

We don't have to be hyper-vigilant in order to be ready for
whatever hill or valley the day will hold. In fact, in that
heightened-awareness state we may find ourselves easily
bombarded with anxiety. Being grateful doesn't blind us to
the realities of life; it helps us endure them with resilience,
grace, and hope. In our alertness, we can be hopeful. We
can know peace, and we can be ready for whatever comes
with the gift of gratitude as our grounding practice.

*Name five things you are thankful for today. If you are
reading this at the start of your day, bring that intention with
you to find five things throughout the day. If this is the end of
your day, recall five things from your experiences today.*

UNSHAKABLE

Let us be grateful for receiving a kingdom that cannot be shaken, and thus let us offer to God acceptable worship, with reverence and awe.

HEBREWS 12:28 ESV

Though there is much in this world that shifts and changes, God never does. He is the same yesterday, today, and forever. This can be like an anchor of hope for our souls. When we don't know what to be grateful for, the unchanging character of God is a good place to start.

We have fellowship with God through his Spirit. This isn't something that is reserved for another time; it is accessible now. The Spirit of God makes his home in our hearts as we open them to Christ. His powerful peace is our portion today and every day. His loyal love never leaves us. His delight in us and his joy for us are ours to feast upon. What a God we have, and what a powerful place of rest we find in his presence!

What do you need most today: peace, patience, or kindness? Whatever you need, God offers it to you freely through his fellowship. Take what you need and thank him for his abundant presence.

ALL DAY LONG

The LORD's name should be praised
from where the sun rises to where it sets.

PSALM 113:3 NCV

In every corner of the world there are a multitude of reasons to give thanks. From the moment the sun rises in the morning until after it sets, through the bright and blustery days as well as the quietude and darkness of night, there are opportunities to be grateful.

The more we practice gratitude, the more naturally we turn to it. This brings a variety of benefits into our lives. It shifts our perspectives and allows us to see the positives. It helps us feel closer to the people in our lives. It increases our patience and makes transitions a bit smoother. Through everything, the one who created us remains the same. He has given us so many reasons to praise him, not the least of which is his lavish love.

Intentionally give thanks for something whenever gratitude comes to mind today. Turn your attentions near and far toward gratitude!

WHERE THE SPIRIT IS

Where can I go from Your Spirit?
Or where can I flee from Your presence?

PSALM 139:7 NASB

There is no place so remote that we are without the presence of God. We are never without goodness. Even in the middle of the ocean, we can find reasons to give thanks. Where the Spirit of the Lord is, there is peace, joy, love, hope, and freedom. It is easy to think that when we move ahead in areas of our lives we will experience greater satisfaction, but the problem with that assumption is that there actually is no end point. Once we get to what we thought "it" was, the mark moves to some other goal.

The practice of gratitude helps us connect with the goodness that is already with us. We will not experience deeper satisfaction in life by ignoring the beauty that is ours now. We may look back with hindsight and wish for what we have now. Gratitude encourages us to embrace the present in a way that leads to deeper contentment no matter what the season or where place we are in the moment.

Ask the Lord to open your eyes to the fulfilled promises where you are already living. Note them in a place you can come back to when you need the reminder.

EVIDENCE OF HOPE

God has proved his love by giving us his greatest treasure, the gift of his Son. And since God freely offered him up as the sacrifice for us all, he certainly won't withhold from us anything else he has to give.

ROMANS 8:32 TPT

Christ's sacrifice opened the door into God's presence. We can come to him with all our baggage and lay it down before him; we don't have to carry it any longer. In his presence, we find rest for our souls and an invitation to peace, joy, and love. There is more in his heart for us than we can imagine!

When we need a fresh dose of hope, sometimes what we really need is to know that we are seen. We matter. We are loved. God is not done with us. He has not run out of marvelous mercy to restore what we feel is long gone. He is better than we know, and he is available to us with his love right now. There is an abundance in him, and we never need to stay away from our Father. With gratitude, let's enter his courts with thanksgiving and his presence with praise!

Think about the last time you felt a glimmer of hope in your heart. What caused it? Turn prayerfully to God today and ask for eyes to see where he is already moving in mercy for you.

ONE THING AT A TIME

"If a man has a hundred sheep and one of them gets lost,
what will he do? Won't he leave the ninety-nine others in
the wilderness and go to search for the one that is lost until
he finds it?"

LUKE 15:4 NLT

God watches over all, and still he is concerned with the
one. He does not overlook the smallest details. He is fully
capable of caring for us in our need, and he even goes to
search for those who wander. There is nowhere we can
escape from his Spirit. This is not a warning but a lifeline!

Gratitude helps us notice the details in our lives. Sometimes
getting specific is what our hearts need to feel connected to
hope. We are not made to spread ourselves too thinly over
many responsibilities. We can prioritize what needs to be
done and what values we want to uphold. Then we can let
the pressure go to God for our schedules and the tasks that
fill it. That emphasis in our daily lives will keep us from
wandering.

*Spend a few minutes connecting in gratitude to what matters
most here and now. As you do, set your intentions for the day
and establish your priorities accordingly.*

PERSISTENT PEACE

"Peace I leave with you; my peace I give you.
I do not give to you as the world gives.
Do not let your hearts be troubled and do not be afraid."

JOHN 14:27 NIV

Peace is something that we can access right now, even if we struggle with anxiety. Gratitude helps us reframe hard experiences and focus on the positives that are present even in the most painful times.

The peace of God is not fickle nor is it easily lost. Even so, when we feel chaos and anxiety set in, we can tune into the peace of God which meets us in the middle of our messes. Often anxiety and worry are based on speculations. If we ground ourselves in what is true and what we know here and now, we can tap into the peace of his presence and get out of the spiral of worrying. Though it isn't a magic pill, gratitude has been shown to help minimize symptoms associated with anxiety by reducing stress hormones in the body. It is well worth it to keep prioritizing gratitude in our daily lives.

When you feel yourself jumping ahead into the negative possibilities of what could be, take a deep breath and turn your attention to the present moment. Name three things you can see right from where you are sitting that brings your attention to this place.

EVERYTHING RIGHT

I will praise the LORD according to His righteousness,
And will sing praise to the name of the LORD Most High.

PSALM 7:17 NKJV

In the end, God will make everything right according to his righteousness. His mercy covers our mistakes and relieves our suffering. His grace is sufficient. We have so many reasons to be thankful. Even in hardship, we can rest in the faithfulness of God. He will do what he said he would, and he won't ever abandon his loyal love.

There is enough grace to go around. You are not working from a deficit, and gratitude helps you to recognize this. As you monitor your thoughts and the way you speak, you can connect more readily to the gifts around you. You may find yourself feeling more blessed and fortunate just for recognizing the goodness in your life. In turn, this practice of gratitude may cultivate more peace in your heart about the future. Everything will be all right, even when times are hard.

Take time to acknowledge what you have sufficient of today. As you do, give thanks for each of these gifts of grace.

SWEET AROMAS

Thanks be to God, who always leads us in Christ's triumphal procession and through us spreads the aroma of the knowledge of him in every place.

2 CORINTHIANS 2:14 CSB

We can learn to tune into our senses in order to engage with the present moment. What do we see, hear, feel, and smell? What are the sensations that bring a sense of expansion and connectedness to our lives? Our practice of gratitude can go past the pages of a journal, outside our cognition, and into the visceral instincts of our daily lives.

Has a scent ever brought you back to a specific memory or person? Smell is a powerful thing that we can associate with people, places, or things. When we engage our senses in a purposeful way, we can use them to guide our feelings of gratitude. Gratitude can be as palpable as the air we breathe and as comforting as the warmth of the sun on our faces. We don't have to drum up some theoretical reason to be grateful when we engage with the beauty that is already around us.

Engage your sense of smell or taste today in your gratitude practice. Burn a candle that you love, take a walk and breathe the smell of the fallen leaves, or savor a meal that tastes wonderful.

WHAT HAS PROVEN TRUE?

"This God—his way is perfect;
the word of the LORD proves true;
he is a shield for all those who take refuge in him."

2 SAMUEL 22:31 ESV

When we recognize the fruit that we are experiencing now which grew from seeds planted in the past, we are encouraged in hope. Even in the hard times there are blooms of truth present. God proves faithful to his Word, and so do people of integrity. Where do you see the evidence of follow-through in your life and with your relationships?

Different stages of life call for different reasons to be grateful. Our priorities when we are twenty do not remain the same as we approach middle age. This is natural! And still, we can feast on the goodness of fulfilled dreams even when disappointment is a part of our stories. If we need a refresher of the promises God has delivered in our lives, his goodness we could not have imagined realized, or just a fresh dose of hope, let's hide ourselves in the presence of God and take time to look at our lives from his perspective.

Look at your life as it is now. Have you experienced a desire being fulfilled? Note what joy that brought to your life, and perhaps the challenges you hadn't anticipated would accompany your fulfilled dream. Choose to be grateful.

DIVINE EXCHANGE

"I will give them a crown to replace their ashes,
and the oil of gladness to replace their sorrow,
and clothes of praise to replace their spirit of sadness."

ISAIAH 61:3 NCV

God consistently offers us his abundance when we are lacking in any area. He gives us strength for our weakness, hope for our despair, and restoration for what we have lost along the way. There is nothing lost in him. He is the fulfillment of all that we long for. He is the perfect portion for every need. We only have to lean on him.

Gratitude can lead us to lay down the weight of our heavy burdens and pick up the light load of goodness. Both are treasures. The weight is not burdensome. Instead of drowning in pain, we are lifted and embraced by love. We can see through the haze of suffering with the light that breaks penetrates the darkness. The sun's rays burn off the fog, and so does the light of gratitude make a path through the dense feelings.

Both literally and figuratively, look for where the light shines in your life today.

NOT AFRAID TO ASK

"Until now you have asked for nothing in My name; ask
and you will receive, so that your joy may be made full."

JOHN 16:24 NASB

The practice of gratitude can clarify our areas of actual
need, rather than any perceived need. It allows us to see
where we already have enough, or more than enough.
Gratitude gives us a healthy perspective that allows us
to see the places where we need to invite others in and
ask for help. Practicing gratitude doesn't mean that we
somehow erase the real needs we have. It simply allows us
to approach things with a more balanced viewpoint.

When we are clear about what our needs are, we can
more readily ask for help. It requires recognition and
vulnerability. It isn't bad to spot areas that we just cannot
keep going in our own strength. We need the support of
others, and so do other people. The practice of gratitude
connects us to the areas that are full and the areas that may
need some more attention; we can then view both clearly.

*Don't try to do everything on your own. When you have a
need, ask someone for help. And when someone asks for your
help, jump in!*

OVERFLOWING GOODNESS

May God, the fountain of hope, fill you to overflowing with uncontainable joy and perfect peace as you trust in him. And may the power of the Holy Spirit continually surround your life with his super-abundance until you radiate with hope!

ROMANS 15:13 TPT

Gratitude can help us when life is going well as well as when life is hard. When things are going well, gratitude helps magnify the good things. When life is hard, gratitude helps us heal, hold onto hope, and find meaning in the mundane. We can experience the overflowing benefits of gratitude no matter what is going on in our lives.

There is a phenomenon that happens when we direct our day's focus. The more we are aware of something, the more we notice it. A simple practice will help illustrate this. Pick a color and look for it in the space you're now sitting. Go even further and take notice as it shows up throughout your day. When we bring our attention to a specific thing, our brains look for evidence of it in the world around us. It is also this way with gratitude. The more we look for reasons to be grateful, the more we will find.

Take the practice of today's devotion and look for good things. Notice throughout the day things that bring a sense of joy, hope, and light.

SIMPLE CRITERIA

Let us continue to love one another, for love comes from God. Anyone who loves is a child of God and knows God.

1 JOHN 4:7 NLT

The call to love one another is not a flippant one. It is also not something that we should overlook. The law of God's love covers every part of his kingdom, all his commands, and the very essence of who he is. If we want to be more like God, then we should endeavor to love without boundaries and to choose grace, mercy, and peace over the need to be right.

The gospel of Christ may not be easy to follow, but it is simple. If we clothe ourselves in love and choose to move with that foundation, everything in our lives will reflect God. The practice of gratitude helps us recognize where the love of God overflows in our lives, and it can motivate us to move in kind. Love is not weak; it is the strongest force in the universe!

Think about the ways in which you feel loved. Give thanks for every expression you see. Consider how you can choose to move in love that is practical and shows it to others today.

CHOOSING TO GROW

When I was a child, I talked like a child, I thought like a child, I reasoned like a child. When I became a man, I put the ways of childhood behind me.

1 CORINTHIANS 13:11 NIV

Gratitude is not an immature practice. It connects us to the childlike parts of us in the best way possible. As we grow and mature, we can have bigger perspectives, greater patience, and a greater capacity for spiritual maturity. On the other hand, children are resilient, quick to forgive, and value small, beautiful things. Gratitude helps us reconnect and grow in all these elements.

Choosing to focus on a daily habit of gratitude means that we are committed to our personal growth. The childish things that Paul spoke about in today's verse can be a variety of things. It could entail waiting for others to move on our behalf or maybe a lack of responsibility. It could also be the inability to see nuances in the world around us, so the viewpoint is simple and direct. As we choose to grow in gratitude, we put away immature ways of relating to others and to ourselves, and we take agency over our own lives beginning with our perspectives.

When you feel impatient or closed minded today, take some time to remember that there is goodness here in this moment. Connect to it, give others grace, and move on.

EVEN THOUGH

Though the fig tree may not blossom,
Nor fruit be on the vines…
Yet I will rejoice in the LORD,
I will joy in the God of my salvation.

HABAKKUK 3:17-18 NKJV

There are times when it feels as if everything is going wrong. The car breaks down, we get some unexpected and unpleasant news, or we simply are overloaded by the endless demands that remove any headway toward reaching our goals. It is in these moments when a habit of gratitude can make the most difference. Though troubles come, we remain grounded because there is still goodness here, too.

On good days, it is easy to bring many things we're grateful for to mind. The undercurrent of contentment may carry us through. On hard days when we feel the bite of the harsher seasons in life, it may take more effort. Even still, that effort is worth it. Practicing gratitude can even help strengthen our bonds during stressful times.

When hard days come, don't forget the power of your gratitude practice. Being able to cross one thing off your to-do list can be a reason to be thankful.

RETURN TO SIMPLICITY

"I have swept away your transgressions like a cloud,
and your sins like a mist.
Return to me,
for I have redeemed you."

ISAIAH 44:22 CSB

Shame can keep us stuck in cycles of destruction, but gratitude can help us see the opportunities of freedom available to us. A simple directional turn, a return to the place where it all started, revisiting a time when we found peace, presence, and joy, can all make the difference. When we reconnect to our values, we can focus and let go of what doesn't serve us well.

Gratitude is a simple yet effective practice in bringing higher levels of contentment to those who practice it. People who can consistently be thankful show higher resilience through challenges, fewer aches and pains, and improved focus. There is so much power in the perspectives we have. Thank God that we can change them! Return to simplicity, return to love, and stop chasing empty pursuits.

What are your core values? What do you want to be true of you? Measure your choices against these qualities and be purposeful about engaging with them.

LINGER IN LOVE

Keep yourselves in the love of God, waiting for the mercy of our Lord Jesus Christ that leads to eternal life.

JUDE 1:21 ESV

Beginning our days by setting our intentions can help us live more purposefully and connect to what matters. It can help us to "keep [ourselves] in the love of God." As we take time each morning to meditate on God's goodness, we grow closer to him. When we decide how we want to engage with others, we can follow through with intentionality.

No matter when we incorporate our gratitude practice, starting our day with a few moments of stillness and turning toward God's love is a wonderful way to set the tone for the rest of it. Regardless of the challenges that might arise during our day, we can ground ourselves in the love that we connected with earlier. We have the grace we need to get us through, and it is more than enough.

For the next several days, spend some time in the morning shortly after you wake up thanking God for the day. Close your eyes, put your hand over your heart, and welcome his love into your day.

SWEET RELIEF

"Let us praise the Lord, the God of Israel,
because he has come to help his people
and has given them freedom.
He has given us a powerful Savior."

LUKE 1:68-69 NCV

When we take time to practice gratitude even for just a few moments, it becomes easier to engage with positivity throughout the day. Studies show that our brains create new connections to help us do this as we put it into practice. Such small steps truly do have an incredible impact on our perspectives.

The palpable feeling of relief when a need is filled can create overwhelming gratitude in our hearts. Let's not forget to thank God and anyone else who blesses us for the ways they make our lives better. In turn, we can fill gaps for other people that we see need to be filled. What a gift it is to bring relief and joy to someone else!

Think of a time when you felt an incredible sense of relief. Thank God for that provision. As you go about your day, look for ways to lend a helping hand to someone who needs it. Let your gratitude lead you into generous actions.

BLESSED COMMUNITY

Praise the LORD!
I will give thanks to the LORD with all my heart,
In the company of the upright and in the assembly.

PSALM 111:1 NASB

It is so important that we allow gratitude to move beyond the walls of our hearts and minds and into the spaces we share with others. Gratitude can be a communal endeavor as well as a personal one. When we share our appreciation with others, they may also be inspired to do the same. One person can set the tone to encourage, especially as we choose to live with that aim in all our interactions.

It is good to give thanks to the Lord, no matter where you're at or who you're with. You can express your gratitude to him in genuine ways by sharing what is on your heart or talking about the power of your practice and how it's helped you.

When you're in a group of friends, coworkers, or with some other gathering, try sharing something that you're grateful for. A wonderful place to start is your gratitude toward others!

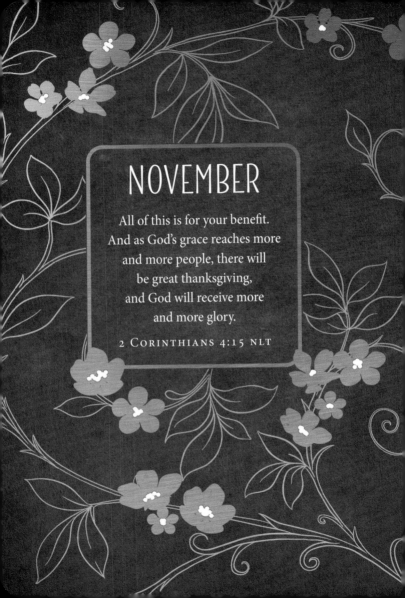

NOVEMBER

All of this is for your benefit.
And as God's grace reaches more
and more people, there will
be great thanksgiving,
and God will receive more
and more glory.

2 CORINTHIANS 4:15 NLT

GREATER UNDERSTANDING

How great is our God!
There's absolutely nothing his power cannot accomplish,
and he has infinite understanding of everything.

PSALM 147:5 TPT

The more we practice gratitude, the more we see reasons in our daily lives to be grateful. Our understanding of goodness and grace grows as we spot miracles of mercy in the middle of our lives.

God has an infinite understanding of everything, as the psalmist told us in today's verse. Nothing stumps him. He is never at a loss for what to do to bring renewal, restoration, and hope. He has all the solutions we need. When we ground ourselves in his goodness and in the faithfulness of his wisdom at work, our trust in his guidance grows. We can lean on him with confidence because he always comes through on his Word. There isn't a promise he has forgotten, and there is no mess we can find ourselves in that he can't lead us out of. He really is greater than we can imagine!

Put a truth you know about God in the forefront of your mind. Ask the Lord to reveal where this shows up in your life and cultivate thankfulness for every answer you find.

COME HOME

> "He returned home to his father. And while he was still a long way off, his father saw him coming. Filled with love and compassion, he ran to his son, embraced him, and kissed him."
>
> LUKE 15:20 NLT

In the story of the prodigal son, the son left his father's home on his own whims and sins, then squandered his inheritance on passing pleasures. In the end, he had nothing left. He decided that his only recourse was to return to his father's house. He didn't expect his father's forgiveness. He was willing to be a servant in exchange for food and shelter. What a surprise and overwhelming grace when the son experienced his father's joy at his return! The father ran to meet his son when he saw him coming. This is how the Father embraces all those who come to him.

It is never too late to humble ourselves and return to where we belong. This may be physical spaces of safety, or it may be spiritual. There is grace for us when we find our way back to the one who created us. Gratitude can help us identify where we feel most embraced, and it can help direct us in our next steps, even if we need to retrace old paths.

Focus on the relationships in which you feel a sense of safety and belonging. Take time to connect with these people and communicate to them the grace that their care gave you.

WHOLEHEARTED APPROACH

"You will call on me and come and pray to me,
and I will listen to you. You will seek me and find me
when you seek me with all your heart."

JEREMIAH 29:12-13 NIV

Gratitude incorporates our focus and our senses. When we turn our attention to what we are grateful for, our whole being benefits from the practice. The more we do it, the more natural it becomes. Just as we bring all we are before God, so can we bring all we are into our gratitude practices.

There is incredible power in our follow-through. Consistency creates results, and that is as true in our commitment to gratitude as in any other area of our lives. It doesn't take much to turn our hearts, but in the practice of it, we make paths for transformation. Let's turn our attention to what there is today to give thanks for. Every thought of thankfulness is a movement toward greater well-being.

Make time in your schedule to incorporate gratitude, especially if you find you do it more then. Consistency builds habits, and good habits can bring greater fulfillment in every part of your life.

ABSOLUTELY ANYTHING

Giving thanks always for all things to God the Father
in the name of our Lord Jesus Christ.

EPHESIANS 5:20 NKJV

There is nothing insignificant when it comes to gratitude. We can be thankful for the way the breeze blows through the trees. We can be grateful for someone lending us a pen to write something down. When we learn to see every act of beauty, generosity, and goodness as fuel for gratitude, we realize that it is possible to give thanks always for all things.

As we go through our day with open eyes, curiosity, and a readiness to respond with kindness, we prime our hearts for gratitude. No matter how mundane the day may seem, as we engage with the bits of light, joy, and peace, we cultivate deep satisfaction for a connected life. This may not sound exciting, but the experience of gratitude is deeply felt for those who practice it. We don't need any changes in our lives to experience this either. We simply need a perspective shift!

As you go into your day, have the intention to give thanks for all the things that you notice which bring a sense of connection. Notice the way the rain falls, the way the trees sway, the way your pet leans into you. It all counts!

SO VERY NEAR

In Christ Jesus, you who were far away
have been brought near by the blood of Christ.

EPHESIANS 2:13 CSB

Gratitude helps us feel closer to those around us, both in
the expression and receiving of it. Whether we share our
appreciation with others or are the ones being thanked, it
can strengthen the bonds of our relationships. When we
feel appreciated, we are more prone to acknowledge others.
When we share our appreciation, we feel closer to the
people in our lives. It is a win-win situation!

If it has been a while since you felt truly seen, it may
help you to be grounded in expressions of love. First and
foremost, you have been created in the image of God by the
power of his love. God beckons you to draw near to him
through Christ. He delights in you and longs for you to
know the life-giving power of his love. As you rest in him,
you who once felt far away from God are brought near to
him. Christ's sacrifice is your covering. Let the Spirit speak
the delight of God's heart over you. You are dearly loved,
and from that place you can be loved to the life he intends
for you time and time again.

*If there is strain in any of your relationships, take a step of
connection by sharing what you appreciate about them.
Express gratitude and see how that softens your heart.*

SHARE THE LOVE

I am acting with great boldness toward you;
I have great pride in you; I am filled with comfort.
In all our affliction, I am overflowing with joy.

2 CORINTHIANS 7:4 ESV

Wouldn't it be a shame if those closest to us didn't know how much they mean to us? Both the pride in a good relationship and the pleasure you get from it should be shared with that special person. When it is, we all benefit. Consider for a moment the relationship between a parent and their child. A good parent encourages their child, makes them feel loved and celebrated for who they are, and creates safe spaces for trying and failing. They can communicate both concern and delight in a way that builds the relationship.

Whether or not we had this type of relationship with our own parents, gratitude can help us connect to real examples of appreciation for people in our lives. We might take for granted that our loved ones know that we love them, but even if they do, it does not mean they don't need to hear it. Open yourself up and share your love with someone today.

Gratitude is a bond-builder. Think of those closest to you and come up with at least one genuine thing you appreciate about them. Share it with them today!

CELEBRATE WHO YOU ARE

You are a chosen people, royal priests, a holy nation, a people for God's own possession. You were chosen to tell about the wonderful acts of God, who called you out of darkness into his wonderful light.

1 PETER 2:9 NCV

No one likes to feel left out. Rejection can make us feel lonely and even question our self-worth. Practicing gratitude can help our feelings in those moments, but it can also help us be gracious with others when we are rejected or neglected.

We can approach hard feelings with curiosity instead of just allowing them to dictate how we feel about who we are. If we feel insufficient, that is a worth issue. The truth is that we are all worthy of love, and not just a little! The overwhelming, grave-busting love of God that surpasses every expectation is the love that reaches each of us without exception. Whether or not we connect to this love is another question. We can celebrate our inherent worth by receiving the love of God and by moving in grace and gratitude. Gratitude helps us connect with our purpose as well as our value.

Be gracious in your interactions today and remember that even though you cannot be everything to everyone, you can know love and love others because of that.

NO BOX CAN HOLD HIM

"Behold, heaven and the highest heaven cannot contain
You, how much less this house which I have built!"

1 KINGS 8:27 NASB

Children are constantly learning and developing. They experience awe, curiosity, and joy in instinctive ways. Just because we grow up does not mean that we can't retain these elements. Though we grow wiser with experience, wisdom does not have to accompany overly serious demeanors.

It is important to realize that we do not know all there is to know. We must remain open to learning, discovering, and changing in life. No one reaches any ultimate destination in any area of life. Gratitude helps us reorient our expectations if we are attempting to reach a destination. Instead, we need to value the place we are at in our journey. Discovery is a beautiful part of life, and if we prioritize gratitude, we will appreciate the wonder that discovery brings. Let's never stop learning about the world, ourselves, others, or God!

Do something for the sheer joy of it today with no purpose other than to pursue delight!

ACTS OF KINDNESS

Let love and kindness be the motivation
behind all that you do.

1 CORINTHIANS 16:14 TPT

Gratitude is a powerful practice that connects us to the positive things in life and helps us focus less on the negative things. Our patterns of thinking change when we make gratitude a habit, and the results are powerful. Grateful people tend to have higher levels of joy, satisfaction, generosity, empathy, and kindness. And the results of practicing gratitude don't just stop with us because others are also blessed as we are loving and kind toward them.

Love and kindness are powerful motivators as our actions become more gracious. We tend to become more patient and generous. We leave more room for people to be who they really are. We are more capable of engaging with the world and offering hope, peace, and encouragement. With gratitude as a starting point, we can lean into the love of the Spirit who is with us now.

Choose kindness in your interactions today. Do something intentionally gracious for someone you may be struggling to understand or like. Even when you are tempted to write them off, choose kindness and love.

BEAUTY IN DIVERSITY

God works in different ways,
but it is the same God who does the work in all of us.

1 CORINTHIANS 12:6 NLT

When we notice God's goodness in the various expressions around us, it can help us see the beauty in diversity. God is creative; we can delight in him by recognizing that there are many different manifestations of goodness and beauty in his creation.

If we wait around for inspiration, it may feel elusive. However, the practice of gratitude is shown to help people be inspired. We don't have to wait for inspiration in order to act. Being inspired works as an incredible motivator for growth, change, and moving ahead. As we look for new reasons to be grateful in our lives, we may just find an inspiration that works like a puzzle piece in helping us see the bigger picture.

As you walk or drive today, look for variety in God's creation. Look at the different ways roads are made, trees grow, people live, and buildings function. Notice anything that inspires or speaks to you. Give thanks for all the different expressions of creativity there are in the world.

POWER OF RESTRAINT

"Watch out! Be on your guard against all kinds of greed;
life does not consist in an abundance of possessions."

LUKE 12:15 NIV

It can be tempting to think that more money will mean
more happiness. The truth is that money cannot buy us
satisfaction. It can't make us more appreciative of the beauty
in life. True enjoyment comes from valuing what we have
right here and now. As we grow in gratitude, we become
more engaged with the people in our lives, and everything
from our relationships to our well-being benefits!

One practical way to practice gratitude is by controlling
our impulses. Before we buy something which we think we
want, take time to truly think it over. Give it a day or two, or
just walk around the store. Delaying gratification can make
us more connected to what truly matters. Instant fulfillment
feels good for a moment, but it quickly fades as we start
to want the next purchase which gives another rush of
dopamine. When we practice self-control, we can put more
agency into our decisions and keep our values straight.

*Practice restraint today in an area of your life that you
usually let go. It may just help you enjoy more of what you
already have.*

ENDURING LOVE

Give thanks to the LORD, for He is good!
For His mercy endures forever.

1 CHRONICLES 16:34 NKJV

When we choose to focus on the unchanging attributes of God, it helps us connect to new reasons to be thankful in our lives. Thinking about God's character one trait at a time allows us to focus our attention on it and how it affects our lives. Consider his patience. Where do you see the gift of patience playing out in your life? How have you benefitted from God's patience and from the patience of others?

Using this as a starting point, choose another attribute of God's nature—holiness, omnipotence, righteousness, creativity, and so on—to recognize throughout your day. Thank him for it, open your heart to him, and look for evidence of it in the world around you, including in the characters of the people you interact with. There are fingerprints of his mercy to be found wherever we look.

For every trait of God's goodness that you spot in the wild today, give him thanks for it.

EMBRACE YOUR LIFE

Let each one live his life in the situation the Lord assigned when God called him. This is what I command in all the churches.

1 CORINTHIANS 7:17 CSB

Living in community with other believers usually entails some very different cultural influences within each family and person. Materialism and competition can thrive in any community; it is our responsibility to guard ourselves against envy and strife. We must each do the inner work of keeping our hearts in check and finding satisfaction in God. Gratitude helps us to do this by making us more connected through our gifts. We don't have to be like anyone else or possess what anyone else has in order to do what God has called us to do.

We are each uniquely gifted. Our personalities and cultures differ, and this is the way God designed it. We can find contentment and cohesiveness in our spiritual practices; we can have confidence in who we have been created to be by cultivating thankful hearts that embrace the variety in our lives and in our situations.

Instead of trying to fit in with others, simply be yourself. Invite people into your home or your activities and allow your differences to be enjoyable as you love each other through Christ.

HOPEFUL EXPECTATION

If we confess our sins, he is faithful and just to forgive us
our sins and to cleanse us from all unrighteousness.

1 JOHN 1:9 ESV

Gratitude can help us clarify what to support, confront, and prioritize. When we are clear on the significant characteristics that require us to raise our voices or to build into our lives, we can then garner the courage to stand firm no matter how others receive us. If we base our actions on whether people accept or support us and our causes, we may never make a move. Or at least it won't feel authentic when we do.

When we understand our own values, we can align our lives with them. Gratitude connects us to what is good and inspiring, but also to that which is personal. What is important to one person may not be important to another, and that's okay. Clarification of our values is a gift, and it is important to operate within those parameters both for ourselves and for the people around us. Our greatest hope is to have clarity for those values that bring us closer to God's love and his peace. In Christ, we are freed from shame and sin. Let's live in that freedom and get closer to true clarity through gratitude.

What does your gratitude practice say about your important values? If you have not done so already, write down your core values. Be sure to base your choices today on them.

THANKFUL FOR THEM

We must always thank God for you, brothers and sisters.
This is only right, because your faith is growing more and
more, and the love that every one of you has for each other
is increasing.

2 THESSALONIANS 1:3 NCV

Our love increases as we express genuine gratitude for each
other. This is one of the most powerful ways that a practice
of gratitude can benefit our lives. If we want to increase our
love, we must be intentional about it. We can't do nothing
and expect a change. We must work toward it; the work of
gratitude has a great return on a little investment.

We must remember that the power of a practice of gratitude
is manifested through the habitual use of it. We may not
experience the benefits as quickly as we want, but it is still
worth following through on. Expressing thanks a few times
will not undo a pattern of mistrust in your relationships.
It will take time to develop the good habit and to show
consistency. Don't be surprised by this. Keep going and
commit to developing growth in this area. It is your work to
do, but you can do it!

*Pay forward kindness and gratitude by doing an act of
service for someone you love.*

RICH IN KINDNESS

In Him we have redemption through His blood, the forgiveness of our wrongdoings, according to the riches of His grace which He lavished on us.

EPHESIANS 1:7-8 NASB

The more gratitude we offer God, the more we can see his kindness toward us. When we look for his goodness, we find it. He is rich in love, and he pours it out on us in both tangible and intangible ways. Gratitude gives us eyes to see where his grace is poured out. It's like light filtering through the clouds. As he shines his light on the landscape of our lives, the treasures of his kindness glint and draw our attention.

There are forgotten and unobserved treasures all around us, but that does not mean they have lost their value. They are waiting to be found. The radiance of God's kindness leads us to see where his mercy already exists in the scope of our lives. We have only to look, and gratitude sharpens our ability to be aware and to find his riches in ordinary places.

Children are drawn to sparkly things! Allow your eyes to see the things that are shiny and investigate them further. Perhaps there is a gift of immeasurable kindness waiting to be found by you as you follow your curiosity!

PERFECT PERSPECTIVE

There is not one person who can hide their thoughts from
God, for nothing that we do remains a secret,
and nothing created is concealed, but everything
is exposed and defenseless before his eyes,
to whom we must render an account.

HEBREWS 4:13 TPT

Nothing remains a secret from God. This can be cause
for worry or for relief. When we seek the Lord with open
hearts, shame has no power over us. God's mercy covers
our mistakes and our failures, and we stand forgiven as we
yield our lives to his love. When we remember that God has
perfect perspective, we can surrender to his goodness. He is
better to us than we are to ourselves; he is gracious and kind.
Let's not keep ourselves from living in the light of his love for
he transforms those who trust in him by generous grace.

When we are inundated by negative news, discouraging
thoughts, and hopelessness, it is important to give those
all to God. When we practice gratitude, we will remember
sooner to turn to him and recognize his goodness.
His mercy meets us in the details of our lives, and our
perspectives transform as we give thanks for the blessings
of his presence.

*Reframe a negative situation by looking for little reasons to
be grateful within, and as a result of, the experience.*

NEW BEGINNINGS

"I am about to do something new.
See, I have already begun! Do you not see it?
I will make a pathway through the wilderness.
I will create rivers in the dry wasteland."

ISAIAH 43:19 NLT

Gratitude can make us more resilient amid change; it can also inspire us to keep moving ahead. Instead of resisting transitions in life, we are more capable of handling grief when leaving things behind. We learn to anticipate with gratitude and expectation whatever is ahead. Grief and hope can coexist, and gratitude makes this a reality for those who practice it.

New beginnings are full of excitement, but that doesn't mean we don't have a moment of hesitation. There are so many unknowns! Still, there is hope as we lean on the goodness of God. Gratitude helps us stay rooted in that goodness which balances out the hard times. Whatever comes, we can trust that the Lord goes with us, he knows what's coming, and we can lean on him through it all.

Continue to root yourself in the gratitude of the present moment. What are three things you are grateful for today? Reflect at the end of the day how that makes you feel about the unknowns of tomorrow.

JUST WHAT YOU NEED

"The Lord is my portion;
therefore I will wait for him."

LAMENTATIONS 3:24 NIV

When we practice gratitude, we teach our systems to slow down. Turning our attention to what is good requires focus. It can't be developed while we're living on autopilot though it may come quicker with time. In the times of waiting, we can ground ourselves with the grace of the Spirit which we have here and now. The Lord is our portion, and he is enough.

You may be surprised by what you have right here in this moment. We all have needs, and many of those have already been satisfied. Don't overlook the basic needs of your own humanity. God is good, his grace is sufficient, and he meets you with amazing generosity.

When you find yourself waiting today at a stoplight, in a line, or simply between scheduled items, allow yourself to meditate on the sufficiency of God in this present moment. Perhaps it helps to ground yourself in practical ways by bringing God's immediate blessings to mind. For instance, "I have water to quench my thirst. I have a chair to put my aching feet on." Whatever comes to mind, give it thought and gratitude.

GIVE A LITTLE

May the Lord of peace Himself give you peace
always in every way. The Lord be with you all.

2 THESSALONIANS 3:16 NKJV

We cannot give away what we do not have. However, we
often overlook what we do have to share. Gratitude gives
us eyes to see the abundance that we already possess
and motivates us to be more generous with that blessed
abundance.

Christ gives out of the abundance of who he is. He is the
Prince of peace, and he offers us a portion of that peace.
He is the Lord of love, and he lavishes his love on us. His
very presence is the grace we need. As we think about the
reasons that we are grateful, we often zone in on the very
areas we can share with others. There is so much goodness
available to us, and whatever we receive allows us to offer
even more to others.

*Identify an area of your life that you have more than enough.
As you do, offer to give to others from that place, whether it
is your time, money, possessions, or service.*

DIAMONDS IN THE ROUGH

Our momentary light affliction is producing for us an absolutely incomparable eternal weight of glory.

2 CORINTHIANS 4:17 CSB

Many precious gems including diamonds and pearls are created under pressure and in the dark. Without darkness and friction at work, they wouldn't exist. The pressures and bleak seasons in our own lives can also create beautiful treasures. When we learn to see the gifts that result from times of affliction, we can endure those times with some hope.

No one can escape the burdens in life. We all will be affected by circumstances that are out of control, but that doesn't mean we will be destroyed by them. The practice of gratitude builds resilience in those who practice it. We cultivate an inner wealth through thankfulness which we can connect to anytime or anywhere. Though we experience pain, we also experience pleasure. There is more than meets the eye at work in the stories of our lives, and gratitude trains our vision to see the goodness amidst the mess.

For every hard thing you face today, find at least three things you can be thankful for to balance out the weight of your experience.

ABIDE

His anointing teaches you about everything, and is true,
and is no lie—just as it has taught you, abide in him.

1 JOHN 2:27 ESV

The act of abiding in Christ means that we are mindfully engaging with him. We align our lifestyles with his values, and we spend time in his presence. We prioritize what he prioritizes, and we feast on his goodness. He is the one who sustains us, feeds, us, and grows us. Through his salvation, we come alive. In his life, we bear the fruit of his kingdom.

How does gratitude connect to this? Very simply, gratitude helps us become more mindful. We reduce our impulse decisions by choosing to redirect our focus. Gratitude is a practice that helps us reframe our viewpoints and slow down our pace. Instead of taking things at face value, we dig deeper. In that process, we can more mindfully choose what we think about and how we engage with the world.

By turning your attention to the presence of God throughout your day, you can be more mindful of aligning your choices with Christ's kingdom values. Whenever you think of it, do just that: breath consciously and remember that God's presence is as close as the air that you breathe.

EVERY TIME

I thank my God every time I remember you.

PHILIPPIANS 1:3 NCV

Our thoughts about the people in our lives affect how we treat them. If we are resentful, that will quickly come through in our actions. If we are tender, that will also shine through. Our actions follow our thoughts, so it's important that we choose our attitudes with wisdom.

Gratitude doesn't eliminate frustrations, but it certainly does help us mitigate them. If we get caught up in petty grievances, we will criticize more than we encourage. Let's do the work of changing the narrative by changing our minds. Of course, this does not mean that we should stay in abusive relationships or unhealthy situations. This challenge is speaking to normal relationship dynamics. If you have someone whom you know you have less grace with lately, try today's practice on them. We can cultivate gratitude in our heart and therefore alter our actions.

Pick one person in your life to focus on for the day. Whenever you think about them, pray a little prayer of thanks for them.

EYE FOR BEAUTY

You are good and You do good;
Teach me Your statutes.

PSALM 119:68 NASB

The practice of gratitude trains our minds to look for the beauty around us. Even when unexpected trials come, we can ground ourselves in the goodness that is still there. Reframing events by being able to see the good can help us be more resilient during them. Beauty is all around us. It is accessible, even in the darkest times.

While it is not a cure for depression, the practice of gratitude can battle the effects of negative thoughts. Those who incorporate thankfulness into their lives experience more positive emotions while benefiting from the reduction of stress-inducing hormones. Though we may not always feel happy in the moment, the practice of gratitude elevates our moods overall. By noticing the beauty in the world around us, we cultivate acknowledgment and thankfulness with an awareness that is simple yet practical.

Take note of every beautiful thing you see today. Don't think about how others perceive it; beauty is in the eye of the beholder! Cherish this beauty and keep your eyes open to finding more.

RESURRECTION LIFE

While we were still enemies, God fully reconciled us to himself through the death of his Son, then something greater than friendship is ours. Now that we are at peace with God, and because we share in his resurrection life, how much more we will be rescued from sin's dominion!

ROMANS 5:10 TPT

The hope of a new life is not just an idea we hold on to. It is found in the cycles of the seasons and the truth of Scripture. There are hints of hope all around even as the days grow shorter and the land rests in the cold winter months.

As we wait for new life to grow, we can still find signs of it. If we are willing to observe carefully with expectant eyes—which gratitude helps us do—we will find reasons to hope. Perhaps the sight of baby bunnies reminds us of the cycle of life. Maybe it's a new leaf sprouting on a houseplant. Any bit of new life and restoration is enough to turn our hearts toward the promise of what is to come. Let's dig deeply and embrace the life we have as well as the life we see coming on the horizon.

Look for signs of new life all around you. Give thanks for each one and remember that they point toward the hope we have in Christ.

MORNING AND EVENING

It is good to give thanks to the LORD,
to sing praises to the Most High.
It is good to proclaim your unfailing love in the morning,
your faithfulness in the evening.

PSALM 92:1-2 NLT

When we start and end our days with gratitude, we build habits that benefit us throughout the ups and downs of life. As we fix our hearts on gratitude in the morning, we instill an intention to embrace the goodness we will find in the coming day. As we look back over the day with gratitude, we ground ourselves in the beauty of the passing moments and refocus our attention on the goodness of God who was with us.

No matter how hard a day is, we can find reasons to give thanks when we look for it. God's faithfulness is always present, and if we have the eyes to see, we will catch glimpses of his mercy meeting us in the middle of the mess.

Do as the psalmist said and meditate on the Lord's unfailing love in the morning and on his faithfulness in the evening.

LIGHT AT THE END

"God's dwelling place is now among the people, and he
will dwell with them… 'He will wipe every tear from their
eyes. There will be no more death' or mourning or crying or
pain, for the old order of things has passed away."

REVELATION 21:3-4 NIV

We cannot escape the challenges of life, especially when
they close in on us like a dark night. The pandemic was one
such time. Everyone was affected by the shutdowns. Instead
of complaining about how things were done, what if we
retained the gratitude for the little blessings and beauties
that were the result of that time? We observed simple acts of
kindness all over the earth which were poignant and sweet.
We can remain intentional in our acts of kindness if we give
our attention to them. Gratitude helps us do just that.

Our mental and emotional health is as important as our
physical health; they all interplay and affect each other. We
must nurture our minds and hearts as well as our bodies.
Even in the hardest times, there are valuable things to
cherish. Through all seasons, we have the promise of God
that one day he will wipe every tear from our eyes and
death, mourning, crying, and pain will be over.

*Prioritize a few moments of silence so you can meditate on
what you are grateful for today.*

DO THE WORK

I saw that for all toil and every skillful work a man is envied by his neighbor. This also is vanity and grasping for the wind.

ECCLESIASTES 4:4 NKJV

Gratitude can make us less materialistic and reduce envy. It shifts the focus from what other people have, to what we already have a blessing. We will not find satisfaction in attaining what others have. We must cultivate joy in our own gardens by tending only them and leaving the grass on the other side of the fence to our neighbors.

We also cannot control how others perceive us. They may look at our lives, see our hard work, and end up wanting what we've cultivated. That is not our fault! We cannot care so much about what others think that we are tempted to neglect or feel guilty for what we have. The truth is, we can only work with what is ours, so let's leave what others think about us out of it. Gratitude can help us do just that.

When you try to bend to others' thoughts about you, take instead a moment to ground yourself in what is specifically yours to do. Focus on the things you are grateful for and reject the vain ambition to please others at the cost of your own integrity.

OPENED UNDERSTANDING

Then he opened their minds
to understand the Scriptures.

LUKE 24:45 CSB

Studies show that gratitude enhances productivity. When we know that our accomplishments are appreciated, we are motivated to work harder. If, however, we don't feel valued for the work we do, we may feel less motivated to impress our employers. "What's the point?" we may think.

Gratitude helps us find our purpose and find meaning in our work. Beginning in our personal practices, we connect with what matters to us. Feedback from others may also help refine our own ideas of what is or isn't important. Let's not overlook the power of gratitude when it comes to our work. If we continue to practice gratitude daily, every area of our life will benefit. Our relationships with our colleagues will be benefitted when we express our appreciation, we become trusted leaders to our co-workers, and we contribute to a healthy work environment.

Consider an area of your work where you have struggled to move ahead. Do you feel underappreciated? Are you confused or overwhelmed by your responsibilities? Look for ways you can connect to gratitude; clarity may just be around the corner.

POWER OF DELIGHT

The LORD your God is in your midst,
a mighty one who will save;
he will rejoice over you with gladness;
he will quiet you by his love;
he will exult over you with loud singing.

ZEPHANIAH 3:17 ESV

When we are delighted in our relationships, the positive emotions of gratitude can make us feel even closer to those who love us. All our relationships— romantic, platonic, and familial—can be strengthened through gratitude. Let's not hold back our delight in others for it paves the way for stronger bonds.

No relationship is perfect, but most can be made better through expressions of gratitude. When a relationship has healthy dynamics, those who receive appreciation for their actions are more likely to return the favor. It does not stretch the imagination much to know that relationships that share mutual value, encouragement, and validation also foster safety, growth, and satisfaction.

Share your appreciation of someone and be specific. Don't hide the joy you have in that person and the delight they bring you.

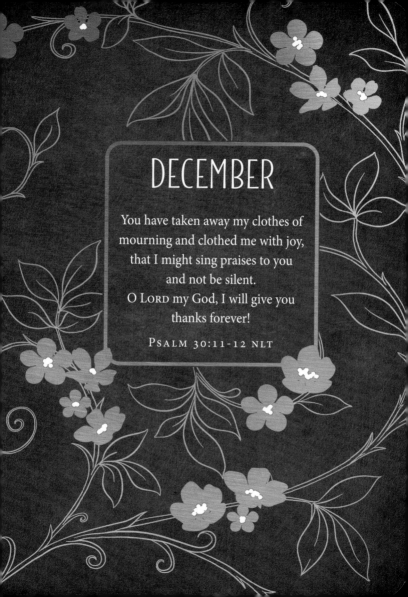

DECEMBER

You have taken away my clothes of
mourning and clothed me with joy,
that I might sing praises to you
and not be silent.
O LORD my God, I will give you
thanks forever!

PSALM 30:11-12 NLT

HOW WONDERFUL

Praise the LORD!
Sing a new song to the LORD;
sing his praise in the meeting of his people.

PSALM 149:1 NCV

At the start of this month as we celebrate the coming of the Lord Jesus as a baby, let's set our hearts on his goodness and our lips on singing his praises. There are many songs that evoke a sense of gratitude and wonder as we consider the gift of Christ's birth. As we gather with other believers this week and this month, let's remember the power of song to unite you in heart and mind.

When we meditate on the wonders of life, we are inundated with the awe of the goodness of God. He is so very good, and he is worthy of our praise. Both alone and in community, let's sing his praises often this season.

Make a playlist of your favorite praise songs to play when you need a boost. May this music give you a strong connection to God and a feeling of wonder and awe with who he is.

FAMILIAR

You scrutinize my path and my lying down,
And are acquainted with all my ways.
Even before there is a word on my tongue,
Behold, LORD, You know it all.

PSALM 139:3-4 NASB

It can be liberating to know that we don't have to explain ourselves to others. Being known well is validation enough. Even when we make mistakes, those who know us well give grace and understanding in their compassionate connections with us. God does this with us, too. He knows us through and through—better than anyone else. What a relief it is to know that he understands us. He loves us, and it is through his love that we receive love, forgiveness, and correction when we need it.

Gratitude helps our own reserves of compassion to grow. As we grow in grace, we can offer others the benefit of the doubt as well as understanding when they fail. Gratitude gives us eyes to see the good parts, so the challenges and frustrations are not all we focus on. Thank God for that! We all can grow in patience, kindness, and love as we practice looking for the goodness in others.

Practice mindful observance of those closest to you today. Look for the things you appreciate and love about them, and then encourage them with those thoughts.

MINISTRY OF RECONCILIATION

*God has made all things new, and reconciled us to himself,
and given us the ministry of reconciling others to God.*

2 CORINTHIANS 5:18 TPT

One of the practical and powerful ways that gratitude
can transform communities is through the ministry of
reconciliation. Gratitude helps us see others through the
eyes of grace, and it moves us in generosity as we become
aware of how much we have that we can share. The practice
of gratitude can help break down walls that are between us
by emphasizing compassion and understanding for others.

No one is excluded from the invitation to dwell in the
kingdom of God. It is up to each of us to decide how we
will live. We cannot force people into the kingdom, but we
can certainly extend the gracious invitation to know God's
love and freedom for themselves. When we share what we
have been given, this is generosity in action, and this is
what Christ has called us to do.

*Meditate on the goodness you have found in your
relationship with Christ. Consider how you can extend this
to others today.*

ADVOCATES OF PEACE

Pray for all people, asking God what they need and being thankful to him. Pray for rulers and for all who have authority so that we can have quiet and peaceful lives full of worship and respect for God.

1 TIMOTHY 2:1-2 NLT

Christ didn't give us any indication that we should fight for our place on this earth or for our own benefit to the detriment of that of others. Instead, he urged his followers to promote and pursue peace. In Matthew 5:9 Jesus said, "They are blessed who work for peace, for they will be called God's children." By practicing gratitude, we can more readily see the things that connect us to one another rather than focusing on the things that divide us.

The more we pray for people, the softer our hearts become toward them. The more we humble ourselves through the practice of gratitude, the more we can see the goodness in the people around us. Let's be promoters of peace, not of conflict.

Pray for the people you struggle to get along with or understand. Pray God's blessing and wisdom over them. Don't forget to rejoice in the quiet and peaceful moments you enjoy in your life, as well.

GREATER THAN BIASES

This is how we know that we belong to the truth and how
we set our hearts at rest in his presence: If our hearts
condemn us, we know that God is greater than our hearts,
and he knows everything.

1 JOHN 3:19-20 NIV

We can rest in the presence of God even when our minds
try to tell us a different story. Have any of us not battled
thoughts that we are unworthy? Yet, it is what God says
about us that matters. He loves us because he loves us, not
because of anything we can do for him. Like a good parent,
he cares for us. Let's rest in his truth which sets us free, for
it is our peace and our liberation.

Gratitude connects us to the truth of goodness, love, and
peace. When we are bombarded with shame, it can be hard
not to spiral emotionally. Even when our hearts condemn
us, though, God is greater than our hearts. The truth of his
mercy is greater than our bad days, and much stronger than
our biases. As we practice gratitude, we can partner with
his truth and see things from a larger perspective.

*If you feel bad about yourself today, remember that God
is crazy about you. He loves you more than you know. Use
gratitude as a touchstone to come back to this truth when
you need it.*

RETURN OF EASE

The threshing floors shall be full of wheat,
And the vats shall overflow with new wine and oil.

JOEL 2:24 NKJV

Gratitude helps us to step outside our conditioned biases and look for alternative ways of seeing things. We don't have to see life as a series of struggles; we can truly go from "glory to glory" (2 Corinthians 3:18) as we look for the goodness that is being produced in our lives now.

As seasons shift and change, we experience times of relief and ease. As summer gives way to autumn, we get reprieve from the harsh heat. As autumn turns to winter, we are invited to rest in the long hours of the cold and dark. As winter gives way to spring, we can embrace the hope of new life growing all around. Though times may feel tough at the moment, there is a change on the horizon. If we keep going, we will know the return of ease to our bodies, spirits, and minds.

We don't have to wait for easier times to connect to peace and rest. We can access that anytime or anywhere through God's presence in our minds and hearts. Gratitude is a fantastic path to his presence. Ground yourself in the moment by bringing your full attention to what you are doing.

SAME MEASURE

"Do not judge, and you will not be judged.
Do not condemn, and you will not be condemned.
Forgive, and you will be forgiven."

LUKE 6:37 CSB

Our actions in the present affect the consequences in the future. What we sow, we will reap. How we choose to treat others will inevitably affect more than simply what that person thinks of us right now. It may create trust issues or maybe it will erode our opportunities for advancement. We may also allow bitterness within our own souls if we refuse to forgive others.

We cannot control what others will do, but we can be judicious about our own approach to life. Gratitude helps us recognize how others have been gracious with us. It helps us get out of our own heads and see how important our relationships are. Gratitude for the people in our lives opens our eyes to see the generosity that has been extended to us and inspires us to be more gracious with those around us.

Notice the things which cause you to make snap judgments. Instead of letting frustrations arise out of things you can't control, look for reasons to be grateful. You can even reframe the feelings you get from certain events and cause yourself to look for reasons to be relieved during them.

GROUNDED VISION

I do not consider that I have made it my own.
But one thing I do: forgetting what lies behind
and straining forward to what lies ahead.

PHILIPPIANS 3:13 ESV

Gratitude inherently connects us to the present as we pay attention to what is good, true, and beautiful around us right now. However, that does not mean that its only benefits are for us today. As we practice gratitude, our focus is refined, and our quality of life increases over time. We have higher hopes for tomorrow when our current day is filled with reasons to be thankful. We neither waste our time ruminating over the past nor fretting about the unknowns in the future.

Gratitude is a powerful practice that connects us to the people around us. We realize that the best things in life are not the material possessions we have but the relationships we have with others. As we cultivate thankful hearts, we are more likely to reach out in compassion and generosity to people. It truly is a practice that benefits everyone.

Look over the length of your gratitude practice and notice the changes in you that have popped up. Are you more patient or kind? Are you more likely to prioritize time with loved ones over time at work? Whatever goodness you find, note it and rejoice, for here is the evidence of God's grace at work in you!

A STORY TO TELL

Thank the LORD because he is good.
His love continues forever.
That is what those whom the LORD has saved should say.
He has saved them from the enemy.

PSALM 107:1-2 NCV

The goodness of the Lord knows no bounds. His love cannot be measured or fathomed. It is abundant, powerful, and present. As we thank God for his goodness, we align our hearts with his kindness and increase our expectations of his wonderful love. He really is better than anyone can ever imagine!

Each of us has a story to tell of the goodness we experience in life; gratitude refines our vision to see the thread of God's mercy within the arc of our own narrative. Wherever we see kindness, faithfulness, and relief, there God is with us. When we experience support, grace, and patience, we experience the presence of God in our midst. Let's not hold back from sharing the stories of his goodness, for we can encourage and build one another up through the power of our perspectives.

Looking back over the last couple of weeks, what stories of relief, peace, joy, and love jump out at you? Write it out as a story you would tell a friend, or if you'd rather, tell it to someone.

EMERGING KINDNESS

The grace of God has appeared, bringing salvation to all people, instructing us to deny ungodliness and worldly desires and to live sensibly, righteously, and in a godly manner in the present age.

TITUS 2:11-12 NASB

When we give our attention to the kind acts of others and the grace of God in the practical moments in our lives, we are also training our minds to look for these blessings. As we do it more and more, it becomes second nature. We really can change our attitudes and thoughts by putting more intention behind them.

As we cultivate gratitude, everything in our lives benefits. Our relationships can be strengthened by focusing on the good in others and sharing our appreciation with them. Our focus and mental clarity are heightened, and our decision-making abilities improve. We become more optimistic, for positive results from a practice of gratitude is not just a theory but is based in reality. There are so many reasons to keep going with gratitude and to develop it into a lifestyle of thankfulness.

Go into your day intending to notice every act of kindness you witness. As you do, consider how you feel after acknowledging each one.

EXPRESSIONS OF LIFE

The Living Expression
became a man and lived among us!
We gazed upon his glory,
the glory of the One and Only
who came from the Father overflowing
with tender mercy and truth!

JOHN 1:14 TPT

Flowers blooming, children laughing, wounds mending—
these are a few expressions in life that bring a sense of
hope, joy, and presence. As you think through what kind of
beauty in both life and nature catches your attention, relish
each as living expressions of God's glory.

Not everything in life is good, but that does not mean
we cannot find goodness in every area of life. As we give
thanks in small ways for the beauty we find, we cultivate
hearts that nourish the life-giving nutrients of hope and
love. There isn't a day that goes by that is without goodness
or beauty; we simply need to acknowledge it in order to
reap the benefits. Gratitude helps us do just that.

Take a walk through your home or workplace and look for
little pockets of beauty, comfort, or joy. Cherish each in your
heart as you notice them.

SHARE THE WEALTH

"Anyone who has two shirts should share with the one who has none, and anyone who has food should do the same."

LUKE 3:11 NIV

In very practical terms, gratitude leads us into being more generous people. When we're not paying attention to what blessings we have, we may not see an opportunity to share with others. Many of us have an abundance of stuff which could benefit those who have less. It's a gift to us as well as others when we give what we don't need.

The practice of gratitude makes us more empathetic. This, too, gives us eyes to see where we might be able to offer a service or a necessary item to others. Gratitude opens the awareness we have of ourselves and others, and it can motivate us to extend kindness in ways that strengthen everyone. We don't need anything more than what we already have in order to practice gratitude and to pay it forward. Instead of putting off lending a helping hand until tomorrow, look for opportunities that arise today to do a good service or gift for someone else.

Go through one room of your house and get rid of everything that is a duplicate or not being utilized. Consider donating to a shelter, someone in need, or a charity.

ALL THINGS WELL

You guided my conception
and formed me in the womb.
You clothed me with skin and flesh,
and you knit my bones and sinews together.

JOB 10:10-11 NLT

When God made us, he did it with creativity and wisdom. He made our brains so they can strengthen and grow not only with natural development, but also by way of practice and intentionality. Through gratitude, we can form new pathways in our brains that lead us to greater resilience in hard times and the ability to see the positives amid the negative aspects of life.

Science affirms what many have known through the experience of practicing gratitude. It can boost your mood, make aches and pains less noticeable, lower your blood pressure, make you more forgiving, strengthen your self-esteem, allow you to sleep better, and more! What wisdom there is in the Scriptures which tell us to thank God. In all circumstances, gratitude benefits us.

Note the specific benefits you have experienced through the time of your gratitude practice. What are some surprising effects? Which have been most impactful to you?

WELLS OF JOY

With joy you will draw water
From the wells of salvation.

ISAIAH 12:3 NKJV

Across the landscapes of our lives, sometimes we need to dig a little to find the springs of joy. As we commune spirit to Spirit with the living God, we gain direct access to the joy of his presence. There is goodness in his peace, love, and life as the Spirit floods our lives with his goodness. Even something as small as a moment of quiet awe can satisfy our souls.

A list of things we are grateful for can help us focus on the impactful ways that God's presence meets us in the nitty-gritty of our lives. There is no joy so small that it doesn't create ripples into our souls. There is no joy so great that we should be intimidated to share it. Every joy builds upon the others in a great display of God's goodness.

At the end of your day, recount every joy, both material and immaterial, that you can remember. Write them down and thank God that his presence is alive and well with you. Don't forget to count the gift of your salvation!

THE HOPE OF DAWN

Because of our God's merciful compassion,
the dawn from on high will visit us
to shine on those who live in darkness
and the shadow of death,
to guide our feet into the way of peace.

LUKE 1:78-79 CSB

God's mercy is in each sunrise, and his grace in every sunset. There isn't a moment when we are without his Spirit even as the darkness sets in. He guides us by his goodness into peace, and he will continue to so throughout our lives.

In the dark days of winter, the lack of light can cause some soulful discomfort. However, darkness does not have to be something we avoid. It is in these short, dark days that we can rest, enjoy a slower pace, be with our loved ones, and cultivate a different kind of gratitude. There are always reasons to give thanks. We can even grow to love the shortened days as we embrace the joys of winter. Consider the blessings of a comforting pot of winter soup, the warmth of our beds, and the opportunity to be close to those we love. Even so, everyday dawns with hope and a fresh opportunity to count our blessings.

Make a go-to list of winter activities, habits, and rituals that bring you joy. When it gets dark outside, light candles, wrap yourself in something fuzzy, and sip a warm drink.

CHOOSING TO REJOICE

Rejoice in the Lord always;
again I will say, rejoice.

PHILIPPIANS 4:4 ESV

Rejoice, and then rejoice some more. That is what Paul encourages the Philippians to do in his letter to them. For every season, for every victory, in every triumph, and through every trial, we can rejoice in the Lord our God who is with us. He never leaves us without the gracious power of his presence. He is always nearby.

It may seem counterintuitive, but rejoicing, even when we don't feel like it, can guide us into feeling like celebrating. Our feelings follow our behavior. Just consider the power of laughter for a moment. Even if you start with a fake laugh, if you do it for long enough it will turn to genuine laughter. Try it! Or watch someone else express a deep, uncontrollable laugh. It catches on as quickly as a yawn. This is a great mood booster and a way to feel lighter in the moment. The same goes for rejoicing. Don't wait to feel like it; simply do it. And then do it some more!

Instead of listing the things you're grateful for today, say them out loud. And don't only say them but say them as if you're celebrating each one! Put a whoop behind it and have excitement in your voice. Even if you don't feel it, act as if you do!

FUEL FOR PRAYER

LORD our God, save us
and bring us back from other nations.
Then we will thank you
and will gladly praise you.

PSALM 106:47 NCV

There are no shortages of things that can frustrate a person, but neither is there a lack of beauty all around us. The things we give more value and thought to all depend on our perspectives. We may think that we value the joys more than the frustrations, but if we spend more of our time complaining than we do being appreciative, then the truth is the opposite. If we want to value beauty more, we must make conscious choices to think that way.

One of the simplest ways of choosing gratitude is to turn our worries into prayers, and to leave them with God. Then we can focus on the good things while not letting the frustrations or hiccups in our day overpower everything else. Let's use the hard times as fuel for prayer and flip the script as we look for reasons to be grateful for what we have.

When you are tempted to complain today, turn your complaints into prayers. As you offer them to God, let your focus turn to what you appreciate about others.

MAKING SPACE

Bearing with one another, and forgiving each other, whoever has a complaint against anyone; just as the Lord forgave you, so must you do also.

COLOSSIANS 3:13 NASB

In order to grow stronger in our relationships, we must be willing to be honest. Honesty leads us to knowing exactly what it is we are dealing with. However, even hard conversations can be laced with love as we show genuine appreciation right from the beginning. As we express appreciation for the person we are talking to, it often changes the mood and softens the space between us.

When we spend time criticizing the people in our lives, they will tend to pull away. No one wants to feel as if they aren't loved or appreciated. Even when we disagree, gratitude helps us to see the value in others. Let's make space for each other through acceptance rather than closing in with criticism.

The next time you need to have an honest conversation with someone involving a conflict or a confrontation, start it out with what you appreciate about that person.

PASSING SHADOWS

> "Who am I, and who are my people, that we could give anything to you? Everything we have has come from you, and we give you only what you first gave us! We are here for only a moment, visitors and strangers in the land as our ancestors were before us. Our days on earth are like a passing shadow, gone so soon without a trace."

1 CHRONICLES 29:14-15 NLT

When we embrace the limited nature of our existence on this earth, it can help us lead more focused, purposeful lives. How we live absolutely echoes into the future and affects the generations to come. There are consequences to our actions and to our intentions. This is one reason why gratitude is so important. It helps us to be clear on what is important and to engage more fully with those very things.

Life is short and we should use the time we have to resolve to be peaceful, loving, and joyful. If we waste our time worrying, we will feel disconnected and unsatisfied with our lives. If we cultivate gratitude, we strengthen our relationship to the present and to the values that are important to us.

Reconnect to your values today and consider what the most important things you want to focus on truly are. Plan your schedule and your days according to these priorities.

GOOD NEWS OF GREAT JOY

The angel reassured them, saying, "Don't be afraid, for
I have come to bring you good news, the most joyous
news the world has ever heard! And it is for everyone
everywhere! For today in Bethlehem a rescuer was born for
you. He is the Lord Yahweh, the Messiah."

LUKE 2:10-11 TPT

Our thinking directs the way we experience life. Perhaps
this is why, when Jesus was born, the news was spread
through angelic messengers. God wanted great expectation
to drive the shepherds' experience. The good news of
the Messiah's birth was a long-held hope for the Hebrew
people. Jesus' birth was the fulfillment of a promise that was
a long time coming.

Proverbs 13:12 says, "When hope's dream seems to drag on
and on, the delay can be depressing. But when at last your
dream comes true, life's sweetness will satisfy your soul."
When at last your dream comes true, there is deep joy and
satisfaction. Let's not let the wait for a deferred hope keep
us from expecting goodness, for it will come.

*Embrace the process you are in, even while you hold out
hope for some goodness to come in the days ahead. Count
every joy that meets you along the way each day and let that
bolster your hope for tomorrow.*

HIDDEN TREASURES

"I will give you hidden treasures,
riches stored in secret places,
so that you may know that I am the LORD,
the God of Israel, who summons you by name."

ISAIAH 45:3 NIV

Gratitude gives us eyes to see the hidden treasures of goodness wherever we are. Even in grief there are gardens of glory being sown. Gratitude trains our vision to spot the glimmers of life wherever it grows. Just because we are experiencing times of hardship does not mean that we need to give in to despair. We can know the relief of God's presence as we cultivate thankful hearts and reframe tough situations through the lens of gratitude.

Gratitude is not delusional. It is rooted in reality, but it may require a shift in our perspectives. Consider how often we talk about the weather. It can be tempting to commiserate about how awful it is, but it won't make us feel any better if we do so. When we look for reasons to be grateful, such as time with our families to play games or a warm and cozy home, it helps us find satisfaction, even in those circumstances when we would normally be aggravated.

Instead of venting about minor frustrations today, commit to finding at least one reason to be grateful. Collect your gratitude treasures throughout the day purposefully.

TRUE FREEDOM

"If the Son makes you free,
you shall be free indeed."

JOHN 8:36 NKJV

When we look expectantly in our search for goodness, joy, and peace, we find it. Christ offers us true freedom. We do not go from being bound to others' expectations to being bound by his. He truly offers us freedom in his love. He knows us through and through, and he loves us completely. His mercy covers our mistakes, and he offers grace to help us in our weaknesses. We never need to fear his reaction to us, for he is patient in kindness and overflowing in wisdom.

All our relationships can be refined and strengthened with the practice of gratitude. This includes our relationship to God, as well as our relationship with ourselves. We don't have to be thankful for everything in order to be thankful *in* everything. Freedom is found as we choose to look for the reasons to be thankful in every season and through every circumstance.

In your practice of gratitude, don't forget to turn to the things that bring you joy. Whether it is a seasonal drink, a talk with a friend, or a warm bath, do something today that lifts your spirits.

RIGHTEOUS KING

Rejoice greatly, Daughter Zion!
Shout in triumph, Daughter Jerusalem!
Look, your King is coming to you;
he is righteous and victorious,
humble and riding on a donkey,
on a colt, the foal of a donkey.

ZECHARIAH 9:9 CSB

Sometimes our greatest gifts come in the humblest ways imaginable. The Messiah did not descend through the clouds; he came as a baby. He did not enter Jerusalem as an adult on a steed; he came on the foal of a donkey. If God himself came in humble circumstances, we can expect to find our greatest gifts in humble packages.

Gratitude gives us the vision to see miracles in the most unlikely places. It helps us to spot beauty in the mundane and gifts of grace in the hard times. As we find encouragement in the little things, we are more apt to be satisfied, rather than chasing after meaning because we are distracted by the next best thing. If the King of kings came to us as a baby born in a stable, then we can find treasures in the wild and insignificant places in our own lives.

When you feel the pull of consumerism or covetousness, remember the humble beginnings of Christ. Look for pleasure and goodness in what is already available to you.

THE TIME HAS COME

When the fullness of time had come, God sent forth his Son, born of woman, born under the law, to redeem those who were under the law, so that we might receive adoption as sons.

GALATIANS 4:4-5 ESV

On Christmas Eve we may find our gratitude flowing easily, or we may find that we have complicated feelings around the expectations of the holidays. With the pressures of family, difficult relationships, and the logistics of accomplishing everything over the next couple days, we may need to adjust our gratitude practice to include moments of silence with God. Connection to him is still the priority even though Christmas is a wonderful opportunity to be with friends and family.

Gratitude can be brought to the forefront of our hearts and minds anywhere and in any situation. As we cultivate the habit, we can more readily turn our attention to the good that is present. Whether we are overflowing with joy or struggling to keep our heads above water, gratitude can be expressed in meaningful ways. It helps us turn our hearts to the Lord.

Be sure to focus on the practical things that you are grateful for today, but don't forget to bring your awareness back to Christ and the incredible gift of salvation we find in him.

WONDERFUL COUNSELOR

A child has been born to us;
God has given a son to us.
He will be responsible for leading the people.
His name will be Wonderful Counselor, Powerful God,
Father Who Lives Forever, Prince of Peace.

ISAIAH 9:6 NCV

Children are a gift. They bring joy and wonder to our lives, and they also require a lot of attention, time, and effort. The joy is real, and so is the exhaustion. To admit one is not to deny the other. More than one thing can be true at the same time. In Christ, we find a powerful God, the Prince of peace, our wonderful Counselor. He is near and he exists outside of our boundaries. As we learn to understand the tension between these diverse truths, gratitude is a wonderful way to grow that muscle.

In hard times as we still find the positive things to connect to, we are strengthening our resilience. We can experience pain or grief but also know joy at the same time. Let's never stop turning our attention to the good that is here and now, for if we keep building habits of gratitude our lives are deeply enriched by it.

For every hard thing you encounter, reach for the good that is still true within each circumstance.

COMPELLED BY LOVE

"God so loved the world, that He gave His only Son, so that everyone who believes in Him will not perish, but have eternal life."

JOHN 3:16 NASB

If we want to lead more fulfilling lives, we need to feel connected to the present day with a clear purpose. Gratitude helps us find meaning in the everyday by bringing our attention to the things that matter. When we only focus on what is going wrong, what remains right may be overlooked and its value is then lost. Truly, what we give our attention to grows, so let's prioritize our practices of gratitude to build strong connections to our purpose.

God is love. He is more than a motivator because love is who he is; it's who the Father, the Son, and the Holy Spirit are. The more we give our efforts into becoming reflections of his love, the more we will be transformed. We start with gratitude; the more we find love's imprints on our lives and in the world, the more we are filled with their influences. The more we are filled, the more we move in the same vein. Love is a force that cannot be measured, but it also cannot be denied!

Love is active. Think of as many acts of love as you can which either someone has done for you, or you have done for them. As you acknowledge them, look for opportunities to spread that through your actions today.

BORN OF GOD

He was not born by the joining of human parents
or from natural means, or by a man's desire,
but he was born of God.

JOHN 1:13 TPT

Jesus Christ was not an accident, and neither are any of us.
Though we may not each be born with the same purpose,
we are born with love's mark on our lives, nevertheless. We
all come into the world with unique gifts to offer. Our very
existence is a miracle! We do not need to beg God to feed
us; he is the greatest caregiver we will ever know.

As you spend time in the Lord's presence today, dare to ask
him what he sees in you. What are the gifts and character
traits he created in you at the beginning? Take time with
an open and thankful heart to hear what he has to say
about you. He is good, and he is full of goodness for you. It
may change the way you present yourself if you know the
specific wonder that he made you to be!

*Gratitude creates greater confidence as we practice it. Write
down all the good traits you see in yourself and thank God
for each one. If you need some help, ask a couple friends
what they appreciate about you.*

CLOSE IN COMFORT

When the Lord saw her, his heart overflowed with
compassion. "Don't cry!" he said.

LUKE 7:13 NLT

Compassion moves us toward one another in love. When
we struggle, compassion reveals that we are not alone,
and we are not without help. Empathy helps us be more
aware of other people's emotions. Compassion is our own
emotional response to this awareness which moves us
to find ways to help. While empathy helps us connect to
others, compassion creates a pathway for that connection.

Gratitude is helpful as we aim to grow in compassion. It is a
powerful thing when we are moved to comfort someone in
their need. When we allow ourselves to feel that compelling
emotion to step in and do something, we should follow
through. Jesus moved in compassion in various ways
through his ministry. In today's verse it was to comfort a
grieving woman, which led to him raising her son from the
dead. Let's not overlook the power of compassion.

*When you feel motivated to help someone today, pay
attention to the feeling and follow through on it. Give thanks
for the opportunity to be the heart and hands of Christ.*

RETURN TO REST

Return to your rest, my soul,
for the LORD has been good to you.

PSALM 116:7 NIV

Studies have shown that those who practice gratitude before they go to bed increase the quality of their sleep. Focusing on feelings of gratitude can help us feel calmer as well as create healing effects within our bodies. Gratitude helps us in a very practical way to have our necessary rest.

If you struggle to settle down at night, perhaps moving your practice of gratitude to your bedtime routine may help. It has been shown that those who do this fall asleep more quickly and stay asleep for longer periods of time. Gratitude doesn't have to be reserved for one time of the day; you can incorporate it as much as you want. Its benefits will help in your waking hours as well as in your sleep patterns. When you need rest for your soul and your body, turn to gratitude.

When you are tired and need a break before going to sleep, turn your attention to those blessings for which you are grateful. It may just be the reprieve your heart, mind, and body needs.

QUIET PLACES

My people will dwell in a peaceful habitation,
In secure dwellings, and in quiet resting places.

ISAIAH 32:18 NKJV

There are many places of respite and refreshment in this world. What is rejuvenating for one person may leave someone else wanting. Through gratitude we can find pleasure and satisfaction no matter where we are; we can also become more aware of what connects us to our own specific goodness in that moment.

We cannot always choose our happy places, but we can certainly become aware of them. No matter where you are in the world, there is a place that is a place of refreshment for you. It may be on the rooftop of a city building where you can watch life moving around you. It may be on a park bench where you can watch people walking by. It may be in a corner of your home where you can curl up with a good book. Quiet, safe places are important for each of us to spend time in.

If you don't already have something in mind, figure out your happy places that give you a break from the world. Every time you are there, give thanks for your safe spaces that give you peace and rest.

A PLAN AND A PURPOSE

"I chose you before I formed you in the womb;
    I set you apart before you were born.
    I appointed you a prophet to the nations."

JEREMIAH 1:5 CSB

Gratitude's benefits are many. It improves our relationships, our outlook on the world, and our sense of self. It can help us be more patient, more positive, and more gracious. We gauge this through our interactions with others, but we cannot forget our relationship to ourselves. This is the longest relationship we'll ever have, so why not improve it?

The practice of gratitude can strengthen our self-image, but it also helps us connect to our innate worth. We are loved, not for what we do or anything we offer, but for who we are. This is what we all long for, and this is what we receive in Christ. There was a plan and a purpose for each of us before we were even growing in our mothers' wombs. When we know the extent to which we are loved and wanted, we can live with that confidence. With humble hearts and a great expectation of God's goodness, we fulfill our lives in Jesus Christ.

Write down all your hopes for the next year, but don't forget to include what you are grateful for through the last one.